Hamlet in My Mind's Eye

South Atlantic Modern Language Association Award Study

Hamlet in
My Mind's Eye

Michael Cohen

The University of Georgia Press
ATHENS AND LONDON

© 1989 by the University of Georgia Press
Athens, Georgia 30602
All rights reserved
Set in Palatino
Typeset by the Composing Room of Michigan
Printed and bound by Thomson-Shore

The paper in this book meets the guidelines for
permanence and durability of the Committee on
Production Guidelines for Book Longevity of the
Council on Library Resources.

Printed in the United States of America
93 92 91 90 89   5 4 3 2 1

Library of Congress Cataloging in Publication Data

Cohen, Michael, 1943-
  Hamlet in my mind's eye.

  (South Atlantic Modern Language Association award
study)
  Bibliography: p.
  Includes index.
  1. Shakespeare, William, 1564–1616. Hamlet.
2. Shakespeare, William, 1564–1616—Stage history.
I. Title. II. Series.
PR2807.C45 1989   882.3'3   88-4773
ISBN 0-8203-1051-4 (alk. paper)

British Library Cataloging in Publication Data available

To My Mother

Hamlet is the tragedy of an audience that cannot make up its mind.

—Stephen Booth, "On the Value of Hamlet"

. . . the most responsive reader will go on to rehearse the play in his mind, considering the text in detail as an actor would, hearing and seeing each moment. Not many commentators write from this point of view. . . .

At this point the reader will become aware of a disconcerting change in his sense of Shakespeare's presence. As a director, he will have had a strong feeling of being in unmediated touch with the author's purposes and "message." As an actor, he will find that this feeling widens and fades. For he will be constantly conscious of the alternatives among which he must choose. The text will now seem more a kaleidoscope than a single dramatic vision.

—Robert Hapgood,
"Shakespeare and the Included Spectator"

Contents

Acknowledgments

I would like to thank the Folger Shakespeare Library for the help and hospitality given me during the preparation of this book, and I am grateful also to the Murray State University Committee on Institutional Study and Research for assistance in the preparation of the manuscript.

Many people have been kind enough to read the manuscript for this book, to offer helpful suggestions for revision, or just to offer encouragement. Among these I wish to thank especially Robert E. Bourdette, Jr., Katharine Cohen, David Earnest, Donald K. Hedrick, Gayne Nerney, Joseph A. Porter, Richard Speakes, Richard Steiger, and Delbert and Edith Wylder. I value the help these have given me, and I treasure their love and friendship.

My thanks also go to the South Atlantic Modern Language Association Study Award Committee and to the good people at the University of Georgia Press.

Introduction

Hamlet is a play of choices. When his mother asks Hamlet to remain at Elsinore, he replies: "I shall in all my best obey you, madam" (1.2.120). How does he read this line? Does he stress the *you*, implying that he is not about to obey Claudius? Does he stress the *best*, implying that Gertrude is directing him to do ill? Does he stress the *obey*, implying that though he will do her bidding, his heart is not in it? Does he stress the *madam*, drawing attention to the formal address and the fact that he is not calling her *mother*, with whatever that may imply about the way she is acting? Or does he read the line without stressing any single word? All these possibilities are there, but on the stage, only one will be given voice.

Every production of *Hamlet* is another interpretation. The person who directs the play, the men who play Hamlet and Claudius, and the women who play Gertrude and Ophelia must all decide on convincing, consistent readings of the main characters. And each reading pushes out other possible readings. If Claire Bloom plays Gertrude as fearful and clinging, she cannot also play her as lusty and independent. This exclusiveness of interpretation creates fewer problems for some parts than for others: the range of possibilities for playing Osric extends only so far, regardless of the actors' maxim that there are no small parts. But as the parts get larger and we approach Hamlet himself, the necessity for one consistent interpretation becomes very limiting.

The simplification inevitable in any coherent stage production would be no problem if there were only one right interpretation of Hamlet's role and each of his speeches. And indeed, some criticism in the past has argued for such a single view. Psychological approaches, historical approaches, and textual approaches (Coleridge, Bradley, Jones, Wilson) have often implicitly asserted that those who find mystery or ambiguity in the play simply do not understand some crucial fact about the main character's personality, the social, political, or aesthetic background of the play, or its printing history. But few critics would take such a position now; most have accepted the pluralism of *Hamlet*, though that acceptance has not always led to favorable critical judgments. One group of critics, which Paul Gottschalk has called the evolutionary school, sees the play's ambiguities as resulting from its sources (Gottschalk 14). Such writers as Stoll, Robertson, and T. S. Eliot, believing Shakespeare's *Hamlet* to be an unresolved combination of disparate elements deriving from several sources, judge the play to be less than a success. Other critics, however, do not find ambiguity or multivalence an obstacle to dramatic success (Schlegel, G. Wilson Knight, Traversi, C. S. Lewis, Mack, Harbage). They may write, as L. C. Knights does, about "the stubborn way in which the play resists attempts at consistent interpretation" (82), but they find such resistance enriching rather than confusing or artistically weakening.

The problem of production remains. Each individual reading of a line contributes to a general effect. A director must choose one reading of an individual line, and his choices for readings of all lines must be as consistent as possible for a unified and coherent interpretation of the play.

But for the reader the play is always in rehearsal. I, as reader, can hold in mind simultaneously all five readings of Hamlet's line above. I can keep in mind many interpretations of Hamlet's character as I move through the play and think not only of how his lines would be read to support one or the other, but how other characters' lines would change and be changed by such interpretations. The following chapters constitute an attempt to read the play according to this plan. I know that reading *Hamlet* in this way begs certain questions about intention in literary works and outrages certain assumptions about intention in dramatic works. I know also that it is more than a little like juggling to hold these various interpretations in mind at once. But I do not know of another way to read such a text that does justice to its recognized multivalence, for what else do critics mean by the play's pluralism (Hedrick 63, Champion 117) if not that there is more than one Hamlet in Hamlet's lines? In fact there are many Hamlets, and several each of the other characters, as *Hamlet* is played on the stages of the mind's eye.

My multivalent *Hamlet* is a reader's play, but it does not therefore follow that I agree with Lamb that there are depths of the title character that cannot be represented on stage (100), nor that I agree with Hazlitt that "there is no play that suffers so much in being transferred to the stage" (237). What a reader can see, a director and an actor can play, but perhaps at the expense of something another reader sees, or the same reader sees at another time, or the same reader sees at the same time. A production can show us only one facet of the jewel at a time.

Even with the singular and explicit interpretation of one theater production there is much of *Hamlet* that still must be played in the mind's eye of the playgoer. For example, Ophelia's description of Hamlet as he appeared to her in her closet (2.1) creates a scene which is probably remembered by spectators of the play as vividly as any onstage action. Our memory of Hamlet "with his doublet all unbraced" is important, and this scene is as much a part of the action of *Hamlet* as if it really did take place onstage. Moreover, during the moment that Ophelia speaks, the theater audience must join us readers and play the scene in imagination. Having recognized this, we may ask just how much of *Hamlet* forces the audience to do what the reader must do—play the scene in the mind's eye. Besides this scene of Hamlet appearing to Ophelia in her closet, the reported scenes include Ophelia's drowning; Hamlet in his sea gown, discovering the treachery of Claudius and the negligent malice of Rosencrantz and Guildenstern; Hamlet in the sea fight; the first appearances of the ghost, described by Bernardo to Horatio and by Horatio to Hamlet; the murder, as described by the ghost to Hamlet; Hamlet before his first shock, as Ophelia describes him in 3.1 and as we glimpse from his own words to Rosencrantz and Guildenstern in 2.2; the slaughter of Priam by Pyrrhus, described by Hamlet and the player in 2.2; and many more such places in the action. Besides such explicitly described scenes, there are others merely hinted at or shadowed by fictions within fictions. We are encouraged to wonder how the actual wooing of Gertrude by Claudius differed from what we see in the dumb show of the play, for example, and the details of Claudius's gaining the throne of Denmark are denied us at the same time as we are teased by his first speech pronouncing his kingship a closed issue (1.2).

Some of the most memorable images from *Hamlet* derive from these "offstage" scenes. Many people cannot imagine the drowning of Ophelia without Millais' painting coming to mind, and Fuseli's drawing of Claudius poisoning old Hamlet (an unlikely stage possibility in which the two wear only capes) is a haunting visualization of that scene. The unstaged *Hamlet* demands its theater, and whatever dramatic heresy the thought represents, its first theater is the mind of the author and its last, that of the reader and spectator.

The plan of this book is very simple. I have tried to apply the views expressed above to a scene-by-scene reading of the entire play. The reading is divided into chapters corresponding to the act division of the Globe edition, and within chapters there are divisions corresponding to scene breaks. My concern with how speeches may be read has led me to look carefully at formal and stylistic aspects of speeches and at the formal structure of scenes as well. I have made general comments about the dramatic construction of scenes at the beginning of each scene commentary, but with the exception of Act Three I have refrained from doing so at the beginnings or ends of acts because act divisions, if they had any significance for Shakespeare at all, cannot be determined in the case of *Hamlet* beyond the end of Act One. I have discussed the scenes of Act Three as a group only because of the startling parallels of their concerns with acting, shows, audiences, and spectators—even though these concerns are also clearly present in 2.2 and 4.1 and, as I argue in the epilogue, in the rhythm and structure of every scene in the play.

I have used Willard Farnham's 1957 Pelican edition for most of my references to the play. Each of the three texts of *Hamlet* has some standing, even the First Quarto. An editor cannot afford to ignore any of the three. An eclectic text based on the Second Quarto is usually considered the best compromise between the claims of the Second Quarto and the First Folio, the two best texts. I have used Farnham's edition for most of my quotations and line numbering, but I have also indicated some places where it is not possible to choose between Second Quarto and Folio readings with certainty, or even with a strong presumption of authenticity. In these cases (2.2.300–304 is a good example, discussed on pages 53–55 be low) strong conviction usually animates an editor's decision about the correct reading, but the conviction is based on perceptions about style, consistency, or literary merit rather than any irrefutable arguments concerning the text. The presence of such difficulties gives *Hamlet* ambiguities even beyond those we meet attempting to interpret undisputed lines.

I refer to productions of *Hamlet* in order to illustrate the range of possible readings for a line or passage, and, it must be confessed, occasionally to make one of my readings seem more credible. I have limited references to those performances which are preserved in some detail in production descriptions, extensively annotated prompt books, films, or videotapes. It has seemed practical to restrict extensive references to productions to the following nine:

(1) In the nineteenth century the most successful American *Hamlet* was that of Edwin Booth, who played the role for thirty-eight years. Charles W. Clarke recorded minute details of Booth's blocking, physical gestures, and inflections during the production in Booth's own theater in 1870. Charles Shattuck used Clarke's manuscript, Booth's notebooks, stage plans, and a number of promptbooks to reconstruct *The Hamlet of Edwin*

Booth (1969), which may be the most complete record of a performance of a single part before the advent of film and videotape. Booth's performance established an American stage tradition for *Hamlet* that lasted half a century, until John Barrymore's performance in the early 1920s, for which unfortunately we have nothing like as complete a record.

(2) John Gielgud played Hamlet, using some of the recently published ideas of Dover Wilson and Granville-Barker, in a production in New York at the Empire Theater in 1936. The play featured, in addition to Gielgud, Malcolm Keen as Claudius, Judith Anderson as Gertrude, and Lillian Gish as Ophelia. Guthrie McClintic directed. Gielgud's *Hamlet* was generally well-received, but some critics found the actor lacking in strength; Gould Cassal's comment that he "omits the bitter wit [of Hamlet] or reduces it to drawing room malice" is typical (34). This production is described in detail in Rosamond Gilder's *John Gielgud's Hamlet* (1937).

(3) The most notable wartime *Hamlet* was probably that performed by Maurice Evans at USO Camp Shows. A full acting version is given in *Maurice Evans' G. I. Production of "Hamlet"* (1947). This production was a modern-dress *Hamlet*, cut drastically to two hours and forty-five minutes, directed by Sergeant George Schaefer. Samuel Messer played Claudius, Mary Adams, Gertrude, Victor Rendina, Polonius, Howard Morris, Laertes, and Janet Slauson, Ophelia. All of the male parts were played by active-duty officers and enlisted men of the United States Army.

(4) Laurence Olivier's 1948 film version, which won an Academy Award, was over three hours long, even though Olivier cut the parts of Fortinbras, Rosencrantz, and Guildenstern completely. The cast consisted of Olivier, Basil Sydney (Claudius), Eileen Herlie (Gertrude), Felix Aylmer (Polonius), Jean Simmons (Ophelia), Anthony Quayle (Marcellus), Stanley Holloway (Gravedigger), Terence Morgan (Laertes), and Norman Wooland (Horatio). Olivier admitted that he was much influenced by the Freudian interpretation of the play. His Hamlet is somewhat priggish, and the camera keeps returning

to Gertrude's curtained bed throughout the film. Olivier begins the action with his own voice-over reading the speech, "So oft it chances in particular men," from the beginning of 1.4, and then announces portentously, "This is the tragedy of a man who could not make up his mind."

(5) Tyrone Guthrie directed the Minneapolis Theatre Company in a modern-dress production of the play at the Guthrie Theatre in 1963. Guthrie, who was also influenced by the ideas of Dover Wilson, used costumes that suggested a location in Europe just before the First World War. George Grizzard played Hamlet, Lee Richardson was Claudius, Jessica Tandy, Gertrude, Ellen Geer, Ophelia, and Nicolas Coster played Laertes. The part of Rosencrantz was taken by Alfred Rossi, who later wrote up this experience of his graduate-school days in a rehearsal diary and promptbook called *Minneapolis Rehearsals: Tyrone Guthrie Directs Hamlet* (1970).

(6) In 1964 Grigori Kozintsev filmed *Hamlet* in Russian from his own screenplay based on Boris Pasternak's translation. Innokenti Smoktunovski played Hamlet, Michail Nazwanov, Claudius, Eliza Radzin-Skolkonis, Gertrude, and Anastasia Vertinskaya, Ophelia. Kozintsev's wide-screen *Hamlet* (147 minutes) uses many exterior scenes—for example the "rugged Pyrrhus" speech competes with the noises of chickens, horses, and dogs in a yard of the castle—and he combines this sort of naturalistic detail with heavy symbolic use of clothes and draperies, fires, mirrors, and water.

(7) John Gielgud's version of *Hamlet* was filmed (also in 1964) in production at the Lunt-Fontanne Theater. Richard Burton played a very strong Hamlet in this production (186 minutes), often called the "rehearsal" *Hamlet* because it was filmed on a bare platform stage with the actors in modern casual dress as if for a rehearsal. Gielgud took the part of the ghost, Eileen Herlie was Gertrude, Alfred Drake, Claudius, Hume Cronyn, Polonius, Linda Marsh, Ophelia, John Cullum, Laertes, and Robert Milli, Horatio.

(8) Tony Richardson directed a film version in 1969 starring Nicol Williamson as an angry young man in the style of John

Osborne's *Look Back in Anger*. The cast included Anthony Hopkins (Claudius), Judy Parfitt (Gertrude), Mark Dignam (Polonius), Marianne Faithfull (Ophelia), Michael Pennington (Laertes), and Gordon Jackson (Horatio). Much of the 119 minutes of this *Hamlet* is in extreme close-up. The ghost is merely a light, with Williamson's voice, directed at his listeners. Critics were especially impressed with the handling of the play within the play (Greenspun 43; Jorgens 34). They were less pleased by Marianne Faithfull's sexy Ophelia and Williamson's lower-class accent.

(9) The most recent production to which I have referred is the BBC/Time-Life Shakespeare Plays television version of 1980. Rodney Bennett directed Derek Jacobi, Patrick Stewart (Claudius), Claire Bloom (Gertrude), Eric Porter (Polonius), Lalla Ward (Ophelia), David Robb (Laertes), Robert Swann (Horatio), and Ian Charleson (Fortinbras) in this videotape of an essentially complete text of *Hamlet*, running approximately four hours.

Films have their own conventions, different from those of the stage, distorting as they do the distance between spectator and actor, demanding background, and tending to reify what may be left to the imagination in the theater. But they are accurate records of how lines have been read, and so are helpful in this inquiry. For that is the question asked again and again in what follows: How may these lines be read? The intention is to try to open the play up, to demonstrate its manifold complexity, to show that the actors represent human beings who are making choices as they speak. This reading of the play may be seen as a kind of performance variorum *Hamlet*, or, from a less kindly view, as a kind of bedlam *Hamlet* with a multiple personality disorder. In any case, its intent is not to prescribe the way the play must be performed, but the ways in which it may be read and performed in the mind's eye, always its first and last theater.

Act One

Scene One

Productions of *Hamlet* have occasionally omitted the first scene of the play. Cutting the scene shaves at least ten minutes from a play that runs four hours if the whole text is used. There is always pressure to cut *Hamlet,* and eliminating entire scenes is easier than the careful pruning of lines and passages. Cutting the scene enables the director to open the play with a stage grouping of all the principals, with Claudius's set speech for opening lines; it is very tempting as an audience grabber, especially for a director who may have fears about the ghost scene's lapsing into comedy. Another fear about the ghost could also prompt the cutting of the scene: fear of the ghost's reality. For many directors it would be more convenient if the ghost were less real, more ectoplasmic, more, in fact, of a psychological suggestion than a real spirit from beyond the grave.

If this scene is not played and no ghost appears here at the beginning, there is no independent confirmation of its existence. Each time it appears subsequently, young Hamlet is present. Without the first scene, it is wholly possible to consider the ghost a creature or a projection of young Hamlet's mind, invisible and inaudible to others. His mother does not see or hear it in the closet scene, and there is doubt whether Horatio and Marcellus hear it at the end of Act One, when it cries "Swear!" beneath the stage. Without the first scene, in other words, the ghost can be seen as either a figment of Hamlet's imagination or a product of group hysteria that he somehow induces. This "psychological" interpretation of the ghost becomes very difficult if the first scene remains intact, though it is still possible. For example, the same actor might play the ghost and young Hamlet, in which case this would be the only appearance of the ghost, a disembodied voice taking his lines in the other ghost scenes. I do not know that *Hamlet* has ever been played this way; it is as much a rejection of the text as cutting the first scene entirely.

The scene explicitly destroys the idea of the ghost as "fantasy" or fancy of one or several persons. Marcellus and Bernardo have already seen it twice, and Horatio, who begins as a skeptic, is forced to "approve their eyes" and confirm the ghost's reality, though it will not obey his charge and speak to him. In his book on Shakespeare's opening scenes, Robert Willson says that "conversion from skepticism to belief is the main business of 1.1 of *Hamlet*" (119) and that Horatio's conversion prefigures "the conversion of Hamlet from cynic to believer during the course of the play" (116). This is the first of many places in the play (such as 3.2, 5.1, and 5.2) where Horatio can be seen as the audience's onstage representative, his skepticism mirroring ours, our belief obtained the easier because of his.

The scene accomplishes much more than establishing the ghost's reality, much that is lost if it is cut. It is not, interestingly, an exposition scene in the usual sense. It contains exposition, to be sure, in the discussion Marcellus, Horatio, and Bernardo hold concerning Denmark's preparations for war, but many of those details are repeated by Claudius in his first speech in 1.2. What is important here is not the exposition itself but the mood which is created by the doubt and apprehension of Marcellus, Horatio's description of Fortinbras's challenge, and Bernardo's assertion that the dead king "was and is the question of these wars" (111). If we had only Claudius's version of the Fortinbras matter, we would not suspect it could ever lead to war.

The most potent effect of the scene is the mood it creates.

Francisco's sickness at heart, Horatio's fear and wonder, the strangeness of the ghost and what it may bode, the apprehension and mystery about the very watch the Danes keep, the ghost's silence about its purpose—all these things work on the spectator not only to create suspense and apprehension, but also to ensure that when Claudius comes onstage with his confident, not-to-worry manner, we are not taken in by his dismissal of the danger to Denmark. His treatment of what we have already felt to be a grave threat leads us to question everything else he says, even if his manner did not.

This is much for a scene to accomplish, especially since it does not introduce any principal character, unless Horatio is to be considered one.

Hamlet begins with a question: Bernardo asks, "Who's there?" But Bernardo is the relief rather than the sentry on duty, and Francisco counters, "Nay, answer *me*. Stand and unfold *your*self"—that is, "I'm the sentry; I'll do the questioning; 'Who's there' is my line." But the lines can also read, "Nay, *answer* me. Stand and *unfold* yourself"—that is, "I want answers rather than questions." Francisco asks for discovery and a statement of allegiance. Bernardo stands, in the sense of stopping and also of standing and declaring allegiance, and unfolds by revealing what had been concealed before: his allegiance and loyalties. Neither knows the other at the outset, as the audience knows neither. The mood is of mystery and challenge, and of one who should be challenged (Bernardo) usurping the role of challenger.

Bernardo has come most carefully upon his hour; he is punctual, as is the ghost, returning at the same time as on the previous night. We are made aware of time here—"'tis now struck twelve"—but this time is shortly to be dissolved as the scene moves rapidly from twelve o'clock at its opening to one o'clock thirty lines later to dawn a hundred lines beyond that. As an example of compressed time the scene also works to encapsulate two nights, since the previous night's appearance of the ghost is repeated this night.

There is mystery and also discomfort: it is bitter cold, so dark or otherwise obscure that Francisco and Bernardo cannot immediately recognize each other, and of course, it is frightening, as we are shortly to discover. Is fear the reason Francisco is sick at heart, even though he has had quiet guard? And if it is fear, is it of the physical threat for which the watch has been set or of the less tangible, unknown threat which the ghost poses?

Horatio and Marcellus are challenged in their turn and state, antiphonally, their identities and loyalties. Their entry and approach make another example of time compression, since by the time they reach Bernardo and ask if the ghost has appeared again, Bernardo answers, not that Francisco saw nothing, but that he himself has seen nothing, as if he had been on guard for some time.

To Bernardo's "What, is Horatio there?" Horatio answers "A piece of him." Warburton conjectured that Horatio extends his hand at this line, and other critics have thought Horatio was making a philosophical comment meaning he is not wholly present because he does not agree with the purposes of the watch; he is skeptical, and his heart is not in it (Furness 6). It may be said jokingly—Horatio is not taking any of this seriously until the ghost first appears.

Horatio has been brought along for two reasons: to prove that the ghost is not just the fantasy of Marcellus and Bernardo and to speak to it, since he is a scholar and presumably knows the Latin forms for conjuration and exorcism. Ghosts can be merely imagined, Horatio's skepticism suggests, and therefore his later conviction helps convince the audience more completely. Both Bernardo and Marcellus say that the ghost has been seen by them twice before. Bernardo begins to tell the story of the ghost's appearance, setting the time in imagistic terms (a star returning to the same part of the heavens) and in more prosaic ones ("the bell then beating one"). The ghost's actual appearance renders Bernardo's description unnecessary and is confirmation of it. A visual and dramatic reality fulfills the descriptive preparation for the ghost's entry. Of the ghost's identity a great point is made: it comes in the same figure as the king that's dead. "Looks it not like the king?" "Most like." "Is it not like the king?" "As though art to thyself." Such was his armor, such his frown (43, 44, 58–62).

Horatio, who is a scholar, is supposed to know what to say to the ghost, and his questioning here and at the ghost's reappearance seems to indicate that he has read Lewes Lavater on how to question a ghost. The first thing to do, according to Lavater, is to beseech it in the name of Jesus Christ to tell what it is and to whom it will speak (105). In his first attempt, Horatio asks the ghost's identity and charges it by heaven to speak to him. Its stalking away is suggestive, and can be made more so by Horatio's emphasizing *heaven* in his charge to it. Such an emphasis leads us immediately to ask whether the ghost will be conjured by heaven, and if not by heaven, by what? Hamlet later makes explicit the possibility that the ghost might be an evil spirit which abuses him to damn him. Another possibility, never mentioned, is that the ghost's urging might not be "abuse" in the sense of lies about itself and Claudius as murderer, but that it may well intend to damn Hamlet by counseling the sin of revenge. Hamlet, amid all his questioning, never questions whether revenge might be wrong or anything less than filial duty, if the ghost is an honest ghost. But Hamlet's are not the only questions that might be asked about good and evil.

Again Marcellus reminds us that the ghost has appeared twice before (65). The reiteration of this point (25,33,65) raises some other questions: why does the ghost keep appearing to those to whom it apparently does not wish to speak, if, as appears by the closet scene, it has the freedom of the castle? Why is it armed? Why does it appear at a particular hour each night? Its last appearance, too, was at "the very witching time of night (3.2.373)." Here, too, the previous visits of the ghost are rehearsed, as Marcellus, Bernardo, and Horatio twice sit down to talk and twice are interrupted by the ghost. The rhythm of the scene resembles that of the Banquo's ghost scene in *Macbeth*, but here, everyone can see the ghost.

Marcellus asks a question (69) for our sake and his own:

why is there a watch at all? His words and Horatio's create the impression that there are serious preparations for war, great apprehension, and a dire threat to the country. There is a strict and observant watch, shipbuilding going on day and night, seven days a week, arms making and arms buying. Horatio's answer to Marcellus's question, though it disparages the experience and age of Fortinbras, does not disparage the threat created by Fortinbras's "enterprise":

> which is no other,
> As it doth well appear unto our state,
> But to recover of us by strong hand
> And terms compulsatory those foresaid lands
> So by his father lost; and this, I take it,
> Is the main motive of our preparations,
> The source of this our watch, and the chief head
> Of this posthaste and romage in the land.
>   (100–107)

It should not escape us that Bernardo accepts Horatio's explanation by saying how suitable it is that the ghost appear now, "so like the king / That was and is the question of these wars." (110–11). This fitting connection made by all of them— that the ghost is on state business—is partly wrong. The ghost's business is far more personal, and later he says very little to indicate his concern about the state of Denmark or the ill political effects of Claudius's usurpation.

Horatio's speech about the mote troubling the mind's eye may seem somewhat out of character considering his doubt about the ghost at the scene's beginning. It is in character, of course, for him to bring up the Romans and classical history in mentioning the walking dead and celestial omens preceding Julius Caesar's death. But it is odd that Horatio, a skeptic about the ghost until an hour ago (or is it longer? It will be dawn in another thirty lines), now talks of other omens and signs which have occurred in Denmark recently (121–25).

The ghost returns at 1.1.126. Horatio shows his courage ("I'll cross it, though it blast me" [127]) and his learning, conjuring the ghost to speak to him. The outcome here is ambiguous. Does the ghost fail to speak because of the cock's crowing?

Would the ghost ever speak to Horatio, Bernardo, and Marcellus? Old Hamlet has not hoarded extorted treasure, and he
does not seem to have any foreknowledge about his country's
fate (Horatio's imagining that such foreknowledge might help
avoid something in the future seems a muddled bit of ghost
lore). But Horatio has also conjured it to speak if there is any
good thing to be done which will give the ghost ease and do
grace to Horatio. Does its failure to speak mean that what it
requires would *not* do grace to Horatio? And how exactly
would such an interpretation be conveyed by the actor playing
the ghost?

Before the ghost ever speaks, questions have been raised
about the grace-giving properties—or their opposites—of
what it will ask, as well as about the very nature of its errand.
Is the ghost, armed and stalking the same rounds as the war-
watch, on a public errand? Will it ask of the living actions
which will defend their country or imperil it? Is it on a private
errand? Will it ask of the living actions which will defend their
souls or imperil them?

In the three almost equal speeches of Horatio, Marcellus,
and then Horatio again from line 149 on, the scene relaxes from
the tensions created by the ghost's appearances. There is talk
of dawn, of the wholesome, hallowed, and gracious time of
Christmas, and a particular description of the dawn in Horatio's memorable personification:

> But look, the morn in russet mantle clad
> Walks o'er the dew of yon high eastward hill.
> (166–67)

Horatio suggests that Hamlet should be told what has happened; he is convinced the ghost will speak to him. If the ghost
has state business, why does no one suggest telling Claudius?
There is no hint that Claudius is thought ill of, nor is he unflat-
teringly compared to "Our last king" (80); Claudius's name is
not even mentioned in the scene. He is simply left out of consideration here, as if the "posthaste and romage in the land"
had ordered itself. When we see him first at the beginning of
the next scene, it is without the praise or condemnation that

frequently precedes a character's entrance, though we do have another view of the Fortinbras threat to contrast with the one Claudius will give us.

Scene Two

The second scene introduces all the main characters except Ophelia, whom we will meet in the next scene. This is Claudius's scene for exactly half its length, until the king's exit at line 129; during the first half of the scene he has ninety-two lines to Hamlet's fifteen and Gertrude's nine. Hamlet takes over in the second half of the scene, with eighty-one, or two thirds of the lines. The ritual formality of the opening contrasts with the warmth of Horatio's conversation with Hamlet near the close. There are other parallels and oppositions: ambassadors to another country are sent off at the beginning, while an ambassador from the dead is announced at the end; one young man's wish to leave the country is granted, while another's is refused.

This, the primary exposition scene, works by a series of shocks. We rapidly discover that the present king was brother to the ghost we have already seen, that the king has made an incestuous marriage with his brother's widow, taken over the throne, and apparently gotten away with it without a murmur of opposition. He now seems to be firmly in control and is denying publicly that any real external threat exists for Denmark. He treats young Hamlet with contempt for his mourning and with a kind of vulgarity over their relationships (uncle-nephew and father-son), which not only underlines his incest but will echo in Hamlet's words about their kinship throughout the play. Hamlet's first problem, the death of his father, and his second, the rapid and to him incomprehensible remarriage of his mother, are about to be compounded by the shock that his father's ghost walks abroad. The dramatic emphasis moves, over these first two scenes, from the ghost of old Hamlet to Claudius to young Hamlet, where it will remain, aside from occasional short shifts back to Claudius, until the end of the play.

Claudius's Scene

Claudius begins by telling us that his brother's death is so recent that he and the whole kingdom should still be in mourning. Then he admits to a technically incestuous marriage with his brother's wife, his "sometime sister" (8). This quick remarriage of Gertrude seems to be what has enabled Claudius to climb onto the throne. Shakespeare does not describe how the succession actually worked and whether Claudius's marriage to the queen influenced the nobles to cast their votes for him in the normal process of an elective monarchy or short-circuited any elective process. Claudius also confirms what has been said in 1.1 of the country's danger from without by referring to Denmark as "this warlike state" (9).

Why does Claudius admit these things? It should be pointed out that he goes on to deny them, either explicitly or implicitly, by what follows. That his brother's death is still so recent as to deserve mourning is denied by Claudius's exhortation to Hamlet to stop mourning now that the proper term for "obsequious sorrow" is over:

> to persever
> In obstinate condolement is a course
> Of impious stubbornness.
>
> (92–94)

Claudius implicitly denies that his marriage to Gertrude violates any moral codes by his words to the assembled nobles about how they have freely gone along with this affair. He denies that any serious threat exists to the country by the way he handles the whole matter of Fortinbras's challenge. *Young* Fortinbras has "a weak supposal" of Claudius's worth, which is presumably strong; the state is *not* "disjoint and out of frame;"

Fortinbras's plan is a "dream;" and, rather than a threat, he is a pest (18–25). So much for him.

Part of what Claudius says here is necessary exposition: we need to have other people besides Hamlet talk about how soon his mother's remarriage followed his father's death. Hamlet tends to be confused about it: is it a month (145), two months (138), or two hours (3.2.121)? Horatio confirms that "it followed hard upon" (1.2.179), but he is a friend and in sympathy with Hamlet. Here the antagonist himself confirms that it was quick enough to have the appearance of unseemly haste, quite apart from the unseemliness of its uniting of sister and brother-in-law.

Claudius may be reminding everyone of the unsavory details of his assumption of the throne merely because he can, demonstrating a kind of sleaziness of character dramatically calculated to turn us against him from his first words. He may be doing it because he must, conscience forcing him to address his acts in public and publicly cover them up again. He may also just be ineptly babbling about what has happened without realizing the effect his words may have. The latter interpretation goes along with a reading of Claudius as drunkard, taking off from what Hamlet says about him at the beginning of 1.4. Claudius is rarely played as a drunkard, but much in the text can support this reading. Anthony Hopkins's Claudius, in Richardson's *Hamlet*, came as close to this interpretation as has been done in any modern production. But the whole speech of Claudius here seems nothing if not conscious, deliberate.

The readings that are left concern *policy* or sheer pleasure in exercise of *power*, the one not necessarily excluding the other. For policy, Claudius opens the discussion in order to close it. Once he has announced that those present "have freely gone / With this affair along," he has made it so, even if there was no agreement before. It may even be that there was no formal election of Claudius, in which case he boldly preempted the throne and has now averted the possibility of an election as well. The matter is closed. There will be no further discussion of technical incest or Claudius's right or lack of right to the throne. Now on to other business.

Certainly the handling of the Fortinbras threat seems like carefully controlled policy. The impression Claudius intends to convey is one of control and strength: Fortinbras is not strong enough to present a serious threat; we *are* strong, and moreover prepared; not only can we defend ourselves but we can nip the plan in the bud by exercise of diplomacy; even here we are firmly in control and our ambassadors will do only exactly what we instruct in "these delated articles" (38). But the reader cannot forget that Fortinbras eventually walks into the possession of *all* Denmark, and that Claudius just misses permanent success every time in dealing with threats to his state or himself.

Claudius's very agenda signals control through a careful sense of priority in the items of business he takes up. First, he recaps the question of Denmark's sovereignty (1–16). That settled, he proceeds to external threats (17–41). Next, he moves to the concern of the son of the king's main counselor (42–63). Finally, he turns to personal business of his own—his chiefest courtier, kinsman, and son.

In treating Laertes' business Claudius shows obsequiousness—in the modern sense now—to Polonius, and he does it in a turn of phrase that is distinctive to him:

> The head is not more native to the heart,
> The hand more instrumental to the mouth,
> Than is the throne of Denmark to thy father.
> (47–49)

The same kinds of negative comparatives occur in a later speech—significantly, the first in which we hear Claudius himself refer to his guilt:

> The harlot's cheek, beautied with plast'ring art,
> Is not more ugly to the thing that helps it
> Than is my deed to my most painted word.
> (3.1.51–53)

Claudius is always involved in ironies of representation and rhetoric. An examination of style might at first seem helpful in resolving the matter of how Claudius's opening speech is to be read. With conscious oratory he weighs what ought to be against what is until what is takes over and closes the period: "Taken to wife" (14). Surely this is not the oratory of a drunken sot nor of anything other than a man who knows words can work for him as well as deeds? And yet the speech is curiously close to nonsense. The opposing phrases such as "wisest sorrow" and "defeated joy" (6, 10) eventually seem to cancel meaning. Of course it can be argued that they are intended to obscure rather than illuminate the rather ugly truth of what Claudius is saying, or to anticipate objections.

Hamlet's black costume and usually his stage position put him at the center of visual attention, but Claudius has kept him away from the dramatic center until this moment. Finally Claudius turns to Hamlet. This care, though right policy in showing what should be the king's priorities, also may *appear* to show Claudius's distaste for the coming interview with Hamlet; such a reading is inconsistent with the Claudius who is in full control.and savoring not only power but the ability to rub others' noses in what they must dislike about his having power. But a drunken, unsure Claudius would certainly not relish this conversation with his nephew.

Claudius underlines the relationship: "But now, my cousin Hamlet, and my son—(64)." Claudius is gloating (Hamlet has gone from a rival potentially more powerful than the uncle to a son who was not even considered for the succession and who now is under the uncle-father's control) or he is offering (genuinely or out of policy) peace with the greeting that they are more than kin; Hamlet seems to reject either reading in his response. Claudius then asks a question which denies what he himself has said about the "greenness" of his brother's death: "How is it that the clouds still hang on you? (66)." Hamlet's answer is his first piece of insolence, if we choose to have him read the line that way. This passage, until the king's exit, is as rich in possibilities for diverse readings as any in the play. The first exchange between the two men can be anything from cool to hot, and Gertrude's first speech either a continuation of Claudius's friendly urging or an attempt to bring the temperature down by getting a concession from Hamlet. Gertrude makes two mistakes in talking to her son here. She first says it

is common for men to die—for all that lives must die. Hamlet's
response might be spoken quietly enough: "Ay, madam, it is
common" (74). But it is more than likely that he emphasizes
one of these words, and almost any one of them emphasized
will have the same effect: to imply that Gertrude should realize
that death is common, and will occur to her as well, and to
further imply that she should be acting differently, considering
that fact. The message is the same as that which Hamlet wants
to send in 5.1. when he speaks to the skull of Yorick: "Now get
you to my lady's chamber, and tell her, let her paint an inch
thick, to this favor she must come. Make her laugh at that"
(180–83). His line may suggest that she and Claudius are treating death as *common* in the sense of that which touches only
the common and will not touch them (this is ironic, since they
are talking about the death of a king), but it can also be an
acknowledgment that her remark is merely a cliché.

If Hamlet's reply is spoken kindly, Gertude continues
kindly:

If it be,
Why seems it so particular with thee?
(74–75)

If his response is sharp, she answers in kind, with some impatience. And her answer is the second mistake in that she uses
the word *seems*, which sets Hamlet off; he has been waiting for
some word that denotes dissimulation so that he may un-
burden himself of what he is thinking about the scant mourning duties afforded his father by all but himself. Hamlet's "I
know not seems" (76ff.) speech can certainly be read savagely,
but can it be read any other way? I think it can. A difficult,
inward-looking reading for the actor allows this speech to be
seen as a dutiful response, and one which does not insult all
those present, and especially Claudius and Gertrude. Later in
the scene Hamlet says he is holding his tongue (159), and he
does not in fact say explicitly here that the others are seeming—performing actions that a man might play and only pretending to mourn old Hamlet.

Claudius chooses to put the best construction on this and

Hamlet's following speech (120): they are dutiful, filial sentiments. Claudius's speech (87–117) also has manifold playing
possibilities. Is it avuncular advice of the kind offered to Mar-
garet in Gerard Manley Hopkins's poem "Spring and Fall?" Is it
a genuine attempt to bring Hamlet to his side and have him
look on Claudius as a father? The way Claudius concludes the
scene points to that (121–24). But other things make possible a
different reading. Before he pleads with Hamlet to think of him
as of a father, he has implied that sons should think of fathers
as they would of any trivial sign of mortality in the world, and
that mourning any length of time is absurd, peevish, impious,
naive, simple, and unmanly. Having suggested this about how
relations between fathers and sons ought to be, he makes the
rather equivocal comment, again couched in his negative way:

> with no less nobility of love
> Than that which dearest father bears his son
> Do I impart toward you.
>
> (110–12)

Finally he repeats the sentiment that seems to gall Hamlet so,
that the younger man is both cousin and son to him. Along the
way he has made what seems to be a promise of succession:
"for let the world take note / You are the most immediate to
our throne" (108–109). Claudius's words also function as a reminder to Hamlet that he has been the most immediate to the
throne before.

When Gertrude begs that his mother not be allowed to lose
her prayers (118), is she merely furthering what she takes to be
Claudius's good advice? Or is she saying, in effect, "Pay no
attention to the insulting speech you've just heard from your
uncle-father, but listen to my reasonable request?"

When Hamlet responds (120), his answer depends partly
on the way Gertrude has just spoken to him; the possible variations in this single line are as great as in any other line of the
play, though we will look at only five.

> I shall in all my *best* obey you, madam. [I am not about to
> obey you in what you seem to be counseling, which is
> anything but good.]

I shall in all my best obey *you*, madam. [I am certainly not going to obey Claudius.]

I shall in all my best *obey* you, madam. [But my obedience does not reflect what is in my mind. See line 159, where he says his heart is breaking but he must hold his tongue.]

I shall in all my best obey you, *madam*. [What you ask of me is hardly filial, or the asking maternal. I will not call you *mother*. You have made yourself something less than either kin or kind.]

There is a neutral reading, which Claudius chooses to hear, and in it the *you* may be addressed to either Gertrude or to both her and Claudius. Even this hardly seems a loving reply, though it may be a fair one.

Claudius leaves, as he entered, with a flourish, promising that his cannons and the heavens themselves will announce every time he drinks today. Again there is the intentional doubling of Denmark in his remarks: "Be as ourself in Denmark"— with its irony, since Hamlet has been preempted in any possibility of *being* Denmark, and thus really like Claudius; and "No jocund health that Denmark drinks today"—meaning, "That *I* drink today." Denmark is a thing or place—Hamlet's prison, Claudius's plaything. It is also the king himself. Hamlet cannot be as Claudius in Denmark, cannot be Denmark, cannot escape Claudius in Denmark because Claudius *is* Denmark.

Hamlet's Scene

Hamlet, left alone, speaks his first soliloquy. The speech is one of the most distinctive marks in defining Hamlet for audience or reader, and its ambiguities show the range of interpretation for the character, at least in the play's beginning. This qualification, at least in the play's beginning, is necessary because although we have many possible Hamlets in this speech, the Hamlet of action is missing and does not emerge until Horatio has entered and told his tale. Hamlet begins with self-pity and perhaps self-disgust: the "sallied [sullied] flesh" of the Second Quarto suggests disgust, while the "solid Flesh" of the Folio does not, necessarily. Hamlet moves toward anger, madness and despair, or prissiness, depending on the reading. The movement toward anger will stress those things that Hamlet will finally bring to his mother in a resolution of his anger in 3.4. The reason has failed to govern the heyday in the blood; the beast is in control. Old Hamlet, excellent king and excellent husband, has been replaced by a man who is neither. His mother's action is both an aesthetic and a moral failure, making Hamlet angry and puzzled. The speech concludes with angry condemnation of unrighteous tears, wicked speed, incestuous acts (154–57).

But this speech also provides the first textual evidence for readings which see Hamlet's madness as something more than the deliberate antic disposition he puts on after his talk with the ghost. Here the stress will be on Hamlet's contemplation of suicide, his extension of his mother's perceived grossness to the whole world, the memories of old Hamlet and Gertrude that he cannot get from his mind:

> Heaven and earth,
> Must I remember?
>
> (142–43)

Here also is stressed that mounting hysteria in which Hamlet compresses time so that the two months (if that is indeed the interval, and it seems short enough for impropriety) between his father's death and Gertrude's marriage becomes first a month, then less than a month. And here we must look forward to that point where Hamlet compresses the time to its frightful shortest:

> For look you how cheerfully my mother looks,
> and my father died within's two hours.
>
> (3.2.120–21)

Of course Hamlet may be merely baiting Ophelia here, but if he speaks seriously the line has the force to jog even the most confirmed believers in his calculated madness to a momentary doubt.

For prissiness the speech has much to underwrite the sort

of interpretation Olivier gave to Hamlet in his film version. Hamlet wishes to separate himself from the foulness of the world. He comes close to imaging Gertrude and Claudius as rutting dogs in 150–51. He fills his condemnatory phrases with hissing sibilants: "unrighteous tears," "the flushing in her gallèd eyes," "most wicked speed, to post / With such dexterity to incestuous sheets!" (154–57).

Hamlet's greeting of Horatio is perhaps evidence that Gertrude's behavior is no obsession with him; he will forget himself before he does Horatio, and he has not forgotten himself or his fellow student. Hamlet asks what Horatio is doing in Elsinore (why does he not know?), and the question leads back into Hamlet's preoccupation: his father's funeral, and his mother's wedding, which followed hard upon it. Hamlet makes a joke:

> Thrift, thrift, Horatio. The funeral baked meats
> Did coldly furnish forth the marriage tables.
> (180–81)

How are we to take this remark? How is Horatio to take it? Is it evidence that Hamlet is already resolving his despair with humor, and would successfully grapple with it if he were spared the further revelations that are shortly to come? Hamlet's linking of the funeral and marriage here concisely parodies the labored oxymorons of Claudius's first speech, especially line 12 concerning "mirth in funeral" and "dirge in marriage," but Horatio was not present earlier and only we can appreciate the reference. These lines can also be read with a disgust so profound that it makes the baked meats image begin to reverberate with obscene suggestions. But Hamlet does not wait for a response from Horatio. He continues:

> Would I had met my dearest foe in heaven
> Or ever I had seen that day, Horatio!
> (182–83)

And before we can even respond to these lines, with their revelation that Hamlet does not think killing his enemies is bad enough, but he wants them in hell (a sentiment we will see again at 3.3.76ff.), he alarms Horatio by telling him he thinks he sees his father:

> HAMLET. My father—methinks I see my father.
> HORATIO. Where, my lord?
> HAMLET.   In my mind's eye, Horatio.
>   (184–85)

Horatio describes the three appearances of the ghost—the first two as if he had been there. Hamlet is astonished, and his excitement increases during his questioning of the three men. He shows the peculiarity of mind that Bradley first noted: emotion and excitement sharpen his intellect (158). Even in the midst of strange and troubling news he can test his messengers:

> HAMLET. Armed, say you?
> ALL.   Armed, my lord.
> HAMLET. From top to toe?
> ALL.   My lord, from head to foot.
> HAMLET. Then saw you not his face?
>   (226–29)

Hamlet determines to keep the watch himself, and we see the first signs of his action, resolution, and courage:

> If it assume my noble father's person,
> I'll speak to it though hell itself should gape
> And bid me hold my peace.
>   (244–46)

He swears them, not for the last time, to silence, and they exit. Hamlet voices a suspicion about foul play. He is impatient for the night.

Scene Three

The third scene introduces Ophelia. Laertes says goodbye and gives advice to Ophelia; Polonius says goodbye and gives advice to Laertes and then to Ophelia. Admonitions to Laertes are sandwiched between two sets of admonitions to Ophelia, as the whole scene is sandwiched between two scenes in which Hamlet gets advice from a parent or one who pretends to advise as a parent. But Laertes and Polonius both give similar counsel to Ophelia: be wary of Hamlet. Hamlet gets very different advice in his two scenes: Claudius tells Hamlet to forget his real father and treat Claudius as one, while old Hamlet tells his son to remember his real father and treat Claudius as a murdering, incestuous usurper.

In exposition, the scene informs us that Hamlet has been wooing Ophelia—necessary information which sets up his rejection of her later. This exposition both develops Ophelia's innocent obedience and exposes her father's policy.

The voyage of Laertes has been criticized as of no use to the plot (Benedix 274, quoted and translated in Furness 4:351; Robertson, *Problem* 57–63; Schucking, *Meaning* 54–66), but Shakespeare parallels in Laertes those things which happen to Hamlet and a voyage is one of them, along with the death of a father, an extravagant reaction, the loss of Ophelia, absence from the stage for some time, and ultimate maturity even if only just before death. These echoes of revenger in counter-revenger show us different stages of growth in the main characters.

The scene has few ambiguities by comparison with the two previous ones. Laertes, Polonius, and Ophelia all have a small range of interpretation, however, subtly tied to the way other parts are read. Laertes' interpretation depends to some extent on Hamlet's. To a slighter degree Polonius's depends on Claudius's and Ophelia's on Gertrude's.

The first part of the scene belongs to Laertes, and the problem in reading Laertes is determining how much he resembles his father and how much he parodies him. Another way to put this problem is to ask which of those speeches where Laertes' language resembles that of his father is *conscious* parody. Laertes begins with a warning to his sister that is gentle; he advises her to consider Hamlet's addresses to her as something like puppy love:

> a fashion and a toy in blood,
> A violet in the youth of primy nature,
> Forward, not permanent, sweet, not lasting,
> The perfume and suppliance of a minute,
> No more.
>
> (6–10)

He is willing to admit that Hamlet may indeed love Ophelia now, and without any evil intent, but he warns her that Hamlet may not "carve for himself," but must make a choice that "the main voice of Denmark goes withal." He worries that she will lose her honor or lose her heart. His speech, through line 35, is straightforward, and the natural, domestic, and martial metaphors he employs neither strained nor out of character. But at line 36 he begins a series of *sententiae* (distinguished in the Second Quarto by quotation marks at their beginnings) that are too like Polonius not to be parody:

> The chariest maid is prodigal enough
> If she unmask her beauty to the moon.
> Virtue itself scapes not calumnious strokes.

Mixed with warnings about youth itself is the argument that Caesar's wife (or daughter, or sister) must be above suspicion, and the nature metaphor which follows *does* seem both strained and out of character:

> The canker galls the infants of the spring
> Too oft before their buttons be disclosed,
> And in the morn and liquid dew of youth
> Contagious blastments are most imminent.
> Be wary then; best safety lies in fear.
> Youth to itself rebels, though none else near.
>
> (39–44)

If Laertes is consciously parodying Polonius, Ophelia laughs in response to this; she may laugh even if Laertes is not aware that he is mimicking his father's pomposity. In any case she gives back his advice with a warning to practice what he preaches. Her response to what is Polonius-like in Laertes is one she cannot give to Polonius himself, though she may wish to. These lines at 45–51 are the only indication of possible complexity for the character in this scene. The rest of the time here Ophelia says that she does not know what to think and that she will obey.

One variation (apparently first introduced by Barrymore—Shaw 97) is that presented by Marianne Faithfull and Michael Pennington in Richardson's *Hamlet* (1969). The scene is played as a parting of two lovers, on Ophelia's bed, with words such as "chariest maid," "virtue," and "chaste treasure" assuming great sarcastic force, especially since other parts of the film suggest that Ophelia and Hamlet are lovers also. Richardson's bold presentation makes incest of what in most readings is merely an allowable affection between two comely siblings of similar age, and it fits with the many references to unnatural, multiple relationships in the play pointing to the incest of Gertrude and Claudius: "our sometime sister . . . too much in the sun . . . foul and most unnatural . . . my uncle-father and aunt-mother . . . were she ten times our mother . . . Farewell, dear mother [to Claudius]."

Polonius's parting speech to Laertes is so familiar that we are apt to forget how its matter may bear on anything but our immediate judgment of Polonius as a sententious old man. But "these few precepts" (there are at least eight, and most are double) are presented as advice to a son just before Polonius presents advice to a daughter, and they can be contrasted not only with Polonius's own behavior but with Laertes' later on. Polonius counsels straightforwardness, truth, and the holding of counsel, the value of friends, and the importance of appearance. Polonius has gotten his precepts by heart, although we are not sure from where. Rushton, in *Shakespeare's Euphuism*, suggests Lyly (46); Oscar James Campbell thinks it might be Isocrates in the *Ad Demonicum* (286); but my candidate is the apocryphal book of Ecclesiasticus. That book is also advice from father to son, deals with friends, money, and social situations, and is most dreadfully long-winded.

Laertes being gone, Polonius turns to Ophelia. Polonius is concerned about Ophelia's honor but more about his own; generally he puts his own before hers:

> You do not understand yourself so clearly
> As it behooves my daughter and your honor.
>   (96–97)

He also puts both together, as when he tells her to "tender yourself more dearly, Or . . . you'll tender me a fool" (107–109). The pun combines his being presented to others as a fool (you'll tender—that is *offer*—me [to others as] a fool) with her having a baby (another sense of *fool*). The emphasis, however, is on the dishonor of an illegitimate child to *him*. He is not willing to suppose that Hamlet's intentions might be other than seduction. Roy Walker comments that Claudius's world, which includes Polonius, declares war on true feelings— Hamlet's grief and Hamlet's love (39). Like Laertes, Polonius also uses a martial image to recommend that Ophelia be careful, but significantly it is of parley rather than fight. Like the speech to Laertes, this one too concerns money, but in metaphors of the exchange of currency ("these tenders . . . which are not sterling") and the commerce of the flesh:

> Do not believe his vows, for they are brokers,
> Not of that dye which their investments show,
> But mere implorators of unholy suits,
> Breathing like sanctified and pious bawds,
> The better to beguile.
>   (127–31)

Polonius then returns to "plain terms," forbidding Ophelia to talk to Hamlet, and she promises to obey.

Scenes Four and Five

These scenes play as one, although there is a bare stage and thus technically a new scene at line 91; the purpose seems to be getting Horatio and Marcellus off so that the ghost and Hamlet may have the stage to themselves. This scene confirms fears and suspicions—ours and Hamlet's—and gives the main motive to the action. Only the Fortinbras plot goes on independently until it joins the main and counter-revenge plots at the end; all other actions within the play are affected by the main revenge plot from this point on.

Hamlet indicates at 1.5.40 that he has had some suspicions about his uncle. Ours have come from being privy to the ghost's first appearance and from seeing Claudius in action in Scene Two.

The Ghost's Appearance

Once again we find ourselves on the platform, after twelve, in the cold. Coleridge takes the opening as evidence of Shakespeare's profound knowledge of psychology: men engaged in important and frightening business discuss the trivialities of the weather (2:274). We are reminded of Claudius, before we and Hamlet discover the extent of his guilt, by the trumpets and cannon that celebrate his drinking. It is a Danish custom, though Hamlet suggests it would be better broken than observed. Hamlet says he dislikes the custom because the whole country's reputation is hurt by it; this and the speech it turns into— "So oft it chances in particular men" (23ff.)—show us the other side of a Hamlet who elsewhere is prone enough to generalize, thinking, for example, one woman's weakness that of all women.

The first part of the speech is curious because one cannot tell whether Denmark's reputation for toping is the subject or whether the lines are actually aimed at England. Both can be true. When the madness of Englishmen is talked about later in the play (5.1.140–45), England is talked about *as* England rather than as Denmark. Olivier played this scene very prudishly, and took advantage of a plausible psychological connection between Hamlet's disgust at his mother's actions and his distaste for showy drinking. But Hamlet has greeted his old schoolfellow with "We'll teach you to drink deep ere you depart." He seems to be of two minds about the Danish customs, unless his greeting to Horatio is ironic (perhaps stressing the *we'll*). Here he is partly indignant that the reputation for drunkenness means that an individual Dane will not be taken on his own merits:

> This heavy-headed revel east and west
> Makes us traduced and taxed of other nations.
> They clepe us drunkards and with swinish phrase
> Soil our addition, and indeed it takes
> From our achievements, though performed at height,
> The pitch and marrow of our attribute.
>
> (17–22)

As for the rest of the speech, it seems very serious, and not, like some serious speeches to Horatio, lightened at the conclusion with a joke. Of course, our texts of the speech are flawed, but textual certainty concerning the last three lines before the ghost's entry would not clear up all the questions one is likely to have about it. A historical explanation which Furness cites is that the lines attempt to qualify some of what has been said about Danish drunkenness and were added in deference to Anne of Denmark, the queen of James I. After her death, they could be removed, and thus do not appear in the Folio (Furness 78). Coleridge, a more sensitive reader, suggests that the whole speech helps get away from the mood of uneasy anticipation and makes the ghost's appearance more dramatic and sudden by distracting the audience with abstract reasoning, nice distinctions, and layers of parenthetical syntax (2:275). Coleridge's idea seems sound to me, and perhaps it is no accident that two of the most problematic places in the text come in the involved syntax of speeches by Horatio and Hamlet, each just before the ghost's entry, here and in 1.1.117ff. The question for us is how Hamlet speaks the lines from 17 to 38: frenetically, to stave off the thought of what may be approaching? prudishly, in the Olivier manner? thoughtfully, as thinking of his own shortcomings?

The ghost enters at 1.4.38. Hamlet is afraid and calls on heaven for defense, but he does not hesitate to speak to the ghost immediately, even though he knows the possibility of its wicked intent and origin in hell. Hamlet addresses it in both personal and public terms: "Hamlet, King, father, royal Dane" (Furness says the nineteenth-century acting tradition of the Booths and Henry Irving broke the line after the three increasingly personal terms and then turned to a more general address: "I'll call thee Hamlet, King, father—Royal Dane, O answer me!"—90). He asks why it has come, using an image— a sepulchre with jaws—that unites death and eating. Combined images of food or eating and death occur throughout the play, in, among other places, the funeral baked meats we have just heard of (1.2.180), the poison and posset of which the ghost will speak (1.5.68), Priam's milky head and minced limbs (2.2.466 and 502), the dead Polonius at supper (4.3.17) and my Lady Worm (5.1.82). Most of these images are Hamlet's and predictably equivocal in their manner: they can be read with horror, with disgust, or with grim humor.

When the ghost beckons Hamlet to go with it he determines to follow, though Horatio and Marcellus advise him not to and at first attempt to prevent him. He says he will follow at 1.4.63 and explains why he will not hesitate:

> Why, what should be the fear?
> I do not set my life at a pin's fee,
> And for my soul, what can it do to that,
> Being a thing immortal as itself?
> (64–67)

Horatio's "What if" speech does not address what Hamlet has just said about fearing no harm for his soul and not caring about bodily harm. Horatio and Marcellus attempt to restrain Hamlet and are unsuccessful; he shouts or shakes them away:

> Unhand me, gentlemen.
> By heaven, I'll make a ghost of him that lets me!
> I say, away!
> (84–86)

There are at least two Hamlets in these two dozen lines. One is courageous and unshrinking, Hamlet as Richard Burton played him. He pulls away from his companions, resolute, fearless, perhaps thinking more clearly than they, perhaps merely somewhat prescient in his suspicions about what the ghost has to say. He is not correctly perceived by his companions. The other Hamlet, this one as Derek Jacobi played him, speaks and moves here in a state of overwrought nervous energy, ignoring good counsel, incapable of restraint for other reasons than cool courage. He is accurately fixed by Horatio's "He waxes desperate with imagination" (87). These and all other Hamlets leave the stage with the ghost. Left behind are Horatio, who apparently has taken a quietistic approach, and Marcellus, somewhat more zealous to intervene in saving Hamlet from himself (he seems to have first laid hands on Hamlet at 1.4.80). Marcellus now argues that Hamlet should not be obeyed in his present state, and when Horatio says the issue will be directed by heaven, says "Nay, let's follow him." The two exit.

The Ghost's Message

Hamlet and the ghost return alone. The structure of this scene is like that of Scene Two in that during its first half, while others tell him what he must or must not do, Hamlet mostly listens, occasionally speaking a line or two. Then Hamlet, left alone onstage, speaks a soliloquy, after which he is joined by Marcellus and Horatio. But the emotional level of this scene is much higher, as an authentic and ghostly king reveals truth instead of an upstart and sensual king obscuring it. Hamlet, by contrast with his scornful resistance in Scene Two, is here respectfully attentive and vows obedience. His emotional reaction to the ghost's message is the scene's main variable. He speaks first, either in bold impatience or in the false courage of desperation: "Whither wilt thou lead me? Speak. I'll go no further" (1.5.1–2). And when the ghost demands his attention, he says he will give it, speaking either with fearful or with plain determination. He pities the ghost, who must return to suffering, and expresses surprise at the ghost's mention of revenge; again, either surprise alone or surprise mixed with fear. During the first part of this scene, before the ghost exits and we must begin to deal at least with the possibility of a deranged Hamlet, there are essentially two Hamlets to consider. One is a courageous and dutiful son who wants to know what has happened to his father and what he must do about it. The other is the Hamlet of the Romantics, Goethe's "soul unfit" for the task about to be laid upon it (282). The latter subtends those Hamlets incapacitated for more specific reasons, such as Oedipal guilt for having killed old Hamlet by wishing his death. But every Hamlet is surprised at the ghost's revelation that it has been murdered, and, knowing that, less surprised at the revelation that Claudius is responsible:

> GHOST.   But know, thou noble youth,
> The serpent that did sting thy father's life
> Now wears his crown.
> HAMLET.   O my prophetic soul!
> My uncle?
>
> (38–41)

The ghost's attributes, as has frequently been pointed out (by Robert Hunter West, for example, 61), are a curious and incompatible lot: he is in a Catholic purgatory and yet released at night and fearful of the dawn like a hobgoblin or evil spirit; he is being punished for his sins, yet he counsels revenge; he feels himself wronged by Gertrude as well as Claudius, but he wants only Claudius punished while Gertrude is to be left alone. "The Elizabethans," writes C. S. Lewis, "in general do their ghosts very vilely." He remarks of this one in particular, "It is permanently ambiguous" (11). West argues that Shakespeare "mixed the evidence and did it for the sake of dramatic impact and out of a kind of philosophical reserve from which he seems often to draw some of his impact" (63). The ghost is a dramatic construction whose return to suffering inspires pity, whose disappearance at cock crow or other sign of morning serves to bring us back to the mundane world gently, and whose demand for revenge from beyond the grave gives a kind of sanctity to the plot motive and the revenger which is lacking in the obsessed and bloodthirsty protagonists of *Antonio's Revenge*, *The Revenger's Tragedy*, and other examples of the form.

One of the play's main questions is raised here in the way the ghost speaks of Gertrude's part in these events:

> Ay, that incestuous, that adulterate beast
> . . . won to his shameful lust
> The will of my most seeming-virtuous queen
> (41, 45–46)

The ghost then goes on to describe the details of his poisoning by Claudius. Of what is Gertrude guilty? Had she committed adultery with Claudius before the death of old Hamlet? Did she know about or perhaps even assist in the murder itself? She and Claudius become technically "incestuous" merely by marrying as brother and sister-in-law. The marriage, as incestuous, is no marriage at all and the participants are adulterers. But the ghost may be suggesting more about Gertrude and Claudius before the murder, and this is a question upon which other passages in the play bear: the relation of the murderer and queen in the play within the play, Claudius's confession immediately afterward, and Gertrude's closet scene, all in Act Three.

We are mainly concerned with how these problems affect the way the play is performed and each character interpreted. If Hamlet has taken from his father's words the meaning that his mother was won by Claudius *before* her husband's death, how will a consciousness of his mother's adultery rather than merely of her lustful weakness affect his treatment of her? After the ghost leaves, Hamlet says of Gertrude, "O most pernicious woman!" If he does not now believe her an adulteress, there seems little reason for this remark, since he already knew of her weaknesses. Does Gertrude speak and act differently as a possible adulteress and accessory to her husband's death, rather than merely as a wife too easily consoled for it?

Hamlet's speech beginning at 92 is the first real evidence for the view that he has become *distracted*, in a clinical sense, by the revelations of the ghost. He uses the word himself, about his own head, about the world, or both, at line 97.

O all you host of heaven! O earth! What else?
And shall I couple hell? O fie! Hold, hold, my heart,
And you, my sinews, grow not instant old,
But bear me stiffly up. Remember thee?
Ay, thou poor ghost, while memory holds a seat
In this distracted globe.

(92–97)

It is easy to read the speech in wholly distracted fashion. Another possibility emphasizes Hamlet's rather adolescent dwelling on his discovery "That one may smile, and smile, and be a villain" (108). Yet another has him reading the first lines of the speech (92–95) in rage rather than distracted frenzy, then emphasizing the lines in which he determines to enshrine his father's commandment alone in his memory (98–104), and finally concluding the speech with a grim suggestion, "So, uncle, there you are," that his father is as good as avenged and a reswearing of his oath to remember his father by killing Claudius: "I have sworn't" and, without hearing the entry of his friends, "So be it" to his own oath.

HAMLET.   . . . smiling, damnèd villain!
My tables—meet it is I set it down
That one may smile, and smile, and be a villain.
At least I am sure it may be so in Denmark.
So, uncle, there you are. Now to my word:
It is 'Adieu, adieu, remember me.'
I have sworn't.
HORATIO. My lord, my lord!
MARCELLUS.   Lord Hamlet!
HORATIO.   Heavens secure him!
HAMLET. So be it!

(106–14)

These matters are ambiguous: Hamlet's uncle may be "there" in the sense that Hamlet has written down his observation about villains; Hamlet may have written in his tables what he has said will be alone on the table *of his memory*—his father's commandment. Hamlet's "So be it" may be a fervent or a frenzied amen to Horatio's prayer that the heavens keep the Prince safe (113).

Marcellus's "Illo, ho, ho, my lord" (115) seems an impertinence; one way to make sense of it has Marcellus speaking to *Horatio*, and with the idea that Hamlet will not hear or perhaps understand this reference to a falconer's cry. The two men's state of mind is as at the end of 1.4: they are come to rescue from himself a Hamlet waxing desperate with imagination and not fit thus to be obeyed; they think they need to bring him back to his perch from a too-far flight. But Hamlet, his senses and his mind made keener by excitement, both hears and understands, giving Marcellus back his own phrase and its gloss: "Come, bird, come" (116). Marcellus, chastened, asks "How is't, my noble lord?" (117). He is back in his place, but asking the question, "How is it with you?" that one asks of the mad or the dying.

Hamlet is clearly of two minds in the next lines, wishing to tell his news but afraid that his companions will not keep the secret. He starts to reveal his news about Claudius and stops in midsentence, then continues, making a tautology:

> There's never a villain dwelling in all Denmark
> But he's an arrant knave
>
> (123–24)

Hamlet's concern that the two men will reveal what has occurred seems to come either from fear for his personal safety or apprehension that he might not be able to carry out the ghost's instructions if Claudius is alerted. This concern may be a problem for those who argue that a reason for Hamlet's delay in killing Claudius is the difficulty of public exposure. Hamlet has a chance here for others to carry the word about Claudius's guilt to the court, though he might justifiably fear that they would not be believed, endangering themselves, him, and his purpose.

Hamlet gives Horatio what the latter calls "but wild and whirling words" (133). His intent is either to make Horatio and Marcellus think him mad or simply to tell them they may not. know what has passed:

> For your desire to know what is between us,
> O'ermaster't as you may.
>
> (139–40)

The difficulty with the first interpretation is that Hamlet says he may play a madman (170ff.), so they know his oddness here may be just pose; with the second, that Hamlet *does* let Horatio into his confidence soon—some time before 3.2.74. Hamlet's announcement that he may appear strange or odd and "put an antic disposition on" (170–72) is equivocal evidence in the trial of his real or feigned madness. A man feeling the onset of madness might well say these things; so might a calculating sane man.

Hamlet swears the two to secrecy, and the ghost cries under the stage four times. Both Hamlet and the ghost desire secrecy and urge the oath, but it is by no means certain that the ghost is heard by Marcellus and Horatio. Hamlet assumes they hear (151), but Horatio's words, "O day and night, but this is wondrous strange!" (164) can be played to refer either to Hamlet's behavior of moving about the stage repeating his demand for their oaths or to the commands from the ghost.

Horatio's comment about the strangeness of the proceedings is answered by Hamlet:

> And therefore as a stranger give it welcome.
> There are more things in heaven and earth, Horatio,
> Than are dreamt of in your philosophy.
>
> (165–67)

This response reveals that side of Hamlet which welcomes the new, the exciting, the unheard of. He seems to be, as a man of action and purpose now, expressing scorn for the merely contemplative scholar's view of the world, or for the personal limitations of his friends's view. But this aspect of Hamlet is contradicted by some of the scene's concluding lines:

> The time is out of joint. O cursèd spite
> That ever I was born to set it right!
>
> (188–89)

The speech shows little relish for the surely exciting and novel task before Hamlet. It may show his sense of inadequacy for the task or perhaps a mistaken sense of exactly how much he has been enjoined to do.

Act Two

Scene One

The first scene of Act Two is another divided and symmetrical scene: Polonius gives his attention to Reynaldo during the first half and to Ophelia during the second half. The first part of the scene, with Reynaldo, is often cut, but it is both comic and revealing.

Polonius's methods, like his speeches, are roundabout, including "encompassment" (10), "windlasses," "assays of bias" (65), and indirections (66). Asking a plain question does not occur to him as a way of discovering information. He assumes that which is worth knowing is also hidden and must be got at by circuitous means.

"Give him this money and these notes, Reynaldo"—Polonius begins in generosity and the wish to communicate with his son, or merely furnishes his spy with a pretext. In any case he immediately suggests that Reynaldo interrogate Laertes' acquaintances about his behavior before he visits him (3–4) and that he accuse Laertes (falsely) of "What forgeries you please" (20) in order to draw others into more damning revelations or topping accusations.

There do not seem to be many possibilities for Polonius in playing this scene, except for some nuances of motivation. That is to say, Polonius may possibly be enjoying the prospect of Laertes' transgressions, perhaps even serious ones, in a gleeful, vicarious, and not unfatherly way; this is perhaps the most benign interpretation that an actor can impose on these speeches. It is not too much of a shift in interpretation to see Polonius as jealous rival of his son's pleasures. Still another Polonius, one often played, is the sly old courtier who scarcely thinks of the object of these machinations as his own son; Laertes merely furnishes another opportunity for clever intelligence gathering, and the scene offers a demonstration of what devious measures Polonius has used to get so close to the throne after the drastic recent change. Thematically, the scene shows Polonius in the exercise of unnecessary spying of the sort which will be his undoing by the middle of the play. Polonius is a part of the world that Hamlet has just told us is out of joint; he is at once a result and a symptom of the deceit at Elsinore. But he may be allowed to have many reasons for his part in the general deceit.

Reynaldo's role, with only a dozen partial lines, has yet a nice range of playing possibilities. He can be officious, anticipating his master's instructions and taking them with deference. He can be kindly, but shocked by Polonius's suggestions: "My lord, that would dishonor him" (27). Roy Walker suggests that Reynaldo is shocked at first, but then "delighted with the ingenuity of Polonius's stratagem" (42). He can also be very much aware of what Polonius is like, lending a good deal of irony to the exchange between the two which begins Polonius's farewell:

> POLONIUS.   You have me, have you not?
> REYNALDO. My lord, I have.
>
> (68–69)

Ophelia enters at 74 with her narrative of Hamlet's appearance to her while she was sewing in her closet. The picture we have of Hamlet here "with his doublet all unbraced, / No hat upon his head, his stockings fouled, / Ungartered, and down-gyvèd to his ankle" (78–80) also shows us the inner Hamlet of the play's middle, according to Maynard Mack in "The World of Hamlet." For Mack, Hamlet's "inky cloak" at the play's beginning, his unkempt dress during the play's middle, and his ready traveler's cloak later are all instances of "Hamlet's visible attire giving the verbal imagery a theatrical extension," showing us first the Hamlet of confused mourning, then of distraction, and finally of readiness (511–12).

Whether we agree with Mack's costume analysis or not, we can recognize that Ophelia's description paints a memorable scene, one that is probably recalled by spectators of *Hamlet* as well as many scenes that are acted onstage. There are many such passages in the play which force the theater audience into the same condition as the reader's—that of being obligated to produce the scene in the mind's eye.

To ask how Hamlet's appearance to Ophelia may be played— since the mind's-eye version must include this scene even though the stage version will have only Ophelia's report—is to ask what Hamlet's motives are for appearing as he does. He either anticipates the reaction or he does not. Polonius's immediate reaction is to ask Ophelia whether Hamlet is "mad for thy love?" Ophelia says she fears so.

The premeditating and clever Hamlet knows Ophelia's obedience to her father. He knows she will tell Polonius of having seen Hamlet, that Polonius will probably conclude that Hamlet is mad for love, that he will tell the king and thus disarm official concern over any oddness in Hamlet's behavior. This Hamlet is very clever, but not very effective, as we shall see when we look at how Claudius reacts to Hamlet's supposed madness.

The unpremeditating Hamlet is at once simpler and more complex. He may be genuinely mad—not, probably, for love of Ophelia, at least not that alone, but because of all that has happened to him. It may be that what Ophelia sees and reports is what Hamlet is feeling—pale, not "loosed out of hell / To speak of horrors" (83–84), but fresh from a visitor from purgatory who spoke of them. This Hamlet is disturbed, and his visit to Ophelia not calculated, but impelled by a conscious or unconscious conviction that the beginning of his task means the end of his youthful romance. Hamlet's generalization and extension of Gertrude's perfidy to all women may impel him to see her, look at her, and wonder how one so young, beautiful, and seemingly innocent could be a member of the tribe of Eve (and of Gertrude)—hence the long look, then the nodding of the head, and finally the profound sigh (90–96).

Polonius expresses sorrow (twice) at Ophelia's news and adds what can be, depending on how sympathetically Polonius is played, either a piece of self-realization or another sententious generalization about youth and age:

> . . . beshrew my jealousy.
> By heaven, it is as proper to our age
> To cast beyond ourselves in our opinions
> As it is common for the younger sort
> To lack discretion.
> (113–17)

He and Ophelia hurry to the king.

Scene Two

This is the longest scene of the play, almost six hundred lines from bare stage to bare stage, and almost half again as long as any other scene. It is full of action, beginning with the royal interview of Rosencrantz and Guildenstern, moving to the returning ambassadors, Polonius's theory on Hamlet's madness and his plan to spy on him, Hamlet's baiting of Polonius, his greeting of Rosencrantz and Guildenstern, his welcome to the players, and finally his second soliloquy, in which he chides himself for his delay and reveals his plans to prove the ghost's story by means of a play. Within this rapidly changing action there are episodes such as the discussion of the children's company in London and the speech of Aeneas to Dido on Priam's slaughter, performed by Hamlet and one of the players.

The matter is diverse and the unity of the scene not easily perceived, but we may better see its unity if we look at the scene as essentially one with two parts instead of six or seven. Although the location does not shift, there are two separate spaces where first Claudius and then Hamlet hold interviews. Claudius and Gertrude receive and interview Rosencrantz and Guildenstern, the ambassadors, and Polonius. Hamlet receives and interviews Polonius, Rosencrantz and Guildenstern, and the players. This juxtaposition reveals certain thematic parallels and oppositions among characters. Claudius, whose main intent is to conceal his own guilt and whose secondary intent is to reveal Hamlet's present state of mind, is contrasted to Hamlet, whose main intent is to reveal Claudius's guilt and whose secondary intent is to conceal his own state of mind. Rosencrantz and Guildenstern, the young, outside, amateur spies, parallel Polonius, the old, inside, professional intriguer, spy, and spy-setter. Even the ambassadors and players are parallel groups, sent on their missions because of conflicts or misunderstandings between youth and age, used by the king or by Hamlet for purposes having to do with Denmark's external or internal state, reciting and performing according to "delated articles" (1.2.38) or "a speech of some dozen or sixteen lines" (2.2.526), and successfully performing the task set by Claudius or Hamlet.

The King's Interviews

The scene is not evenly divided; Claudius's business takes up only about a third of the action. Claudius conducts his interviews with great efficiency, and one way to look at him is as successful Machiavel. He has Rosencrantz and Guildenstern fulsomely eager to serve him, his ambassadors report triumphant negotiations with Norway, and his chief counselor reports that he has solved Claudius's most worrying domestic problem, having "found / The very cause of Hamlet's lunacy" (49). But one may also see Claudius here as a man who does not quite have his hands on things. He summons Rosencrantz and Guildenstern to find out what ails Hamlet—or to find out whether what ails him is what Claudius fears ails him—and they end up telling Hamlet their secrets while finding out none from him. Claudius sends ambassadors to Norway to avert danger from Fortinbras, and their mission results, not in the disbanding of Fortinbras's army, but in its strengthening (72–75) and a free pass for it across Denmark, both of which will enable Fortinbras to step into the breach in Danish power at the play's end. He who should be Claudius's wisest counselor is a tedious old fool whose tongue cannot be controlled, who seems intent on alerting Hamlet that he is being spied on, and who seems to be the only one taken in by Hamlet's subterfuges, if that is what they are (if they are not subterfuges, Polonius still mistakes the nature and cause of Hamlet's madness).

The welcome that Rosencrantz and Guildenstern receive from the king and queen seems to promise them—what? Gertrude's words refer to something they can carry away with them:

> If it will please you
> To show us so much gentry and good will
> As to expend your time with us awhile
> For the supply and profit of our hope,
> Your visitation shall receive such thanks
> As fits a king's remembrance.
>
> (21–26)

But both men probably expect advancement of some sort rather than money. The amount of genuine concern for Hamlet's welfare is adjustable. The disclaimers of the two about ambition later in this scene (249–59), their lines about the "cess of majesty" at 3.3.15ff., and their treatment of Hamlet in 4.2 are generally played to make them out to be toadies, but it has been argued that they could hardly act differently, since for them Claudius is the legitimate sovereign (Madariaga 15).

Either Claudius or Gertrude may be played as the person responsible for sending for Rosencrantz and Guildenstern. Claudius can be played as relatively secure, especially since we have not yet seen even the first evidence of his conscience. This Claudius does not fear that Hamlet knows his secret, and he is free from suspicion until the Mousetrap reveals what Hamlet knows. In this reading Gertrude must have been responsible for sending for Rosencrantz and Guildenstern, as we infer from Claudius's restraint and her insistence:

> I beseech you instantly to visit
> My too much changèd son.—Go, some of you,
> And bring these gentlemen where Hamlet is.
>
> (35–37)

Gertrude's interest is not in question, but Claudius may be the one more eager to know the cause of Hamlet's "distemper", out of insecurity and fear or prudence or the desire to retain power over any situation by having accurate intelligence. He, after all, when Polonius says he knows the cause of Hamlet's behavior, responds: "O, speak of that! That do I long to hear" (50). Polonius, however, puts the king off until after the ambassadors have given their news. Whether Claudius suspects otherwise or not, he says—admittedly in the presence of Gertrude, Rosencrantz, Guildenstern, and others—that he cannot dream of any other reason for Hamlet's transformation, "More than his father's death" (8). For her part, Gertrude, alone with Claudius, says of the cause:

> I doubt it is no other but the main,
> His father's death and our o'erhasty marriage.
>
> (56–57)

The "o'erhasty" is a signal of conscience in a squeamish Gertrude, of straightforward honesty in a direct and practical-minded (but still concerned) Gertrude, and in a colder one, merely acknowledgment of a tactical error. But the fact that she does not mention anything further which might be disturbing Hamlet is evidence that she does not know anything further— of murder or even of adultery. It is not conclusive evidence, but it is evidence. On the other hand, though the exchange seems a private one between just the two of them, there might still remain onstage some of the "others" who enter at the scene's beginning, according to the Folio stage direction.

Voltemand reports that the king's business in Norway has gone well. Voltemand's report is straightforward, by contrast with Polonius's to follow. The news he has that Fortinbras's army will be used against the Poles instead of the Danes is welcome, but insures that the Norwegians will appear again, as they have before, as subsidiary drivers of the action. They cause the watch in 1.1, they are Claudius's first piece of official business in 1.2, they seem to show Claudius's effectiveness as king here in 2.2, their march on Poland strikes Hamlet as an example of an ambitious and dangerous effort "Even for an eggshell," at 4.4.53, and their armed force enables Fortinbras to embrace his "fortune" by becoming Denmark's new ruler at the end of 5.2.

Hamlet is a play with an ambiguous relation between public and private concerns, where sometimes Hamlet himself seems unable to decide whether he has been ordered to cleanse Denmark or to extract a purely personal revenge. The repeated appearances and mentions of Fortinbras serve to remind us that Claudius's crime is also an outrage against a state in danger. This iteration will have different effects depending on whether we play Claudius as commanding events or being ruled by them.

Polonius begins to "expostulate" on the subject of Hamlet's madness at 86. Polonius himself repeats the tag, "brevity is the soul of wit" (90), but ironically he cannot be made to shorten his amplifying figures, even though Gertrude demands "More matter, with less art" (95). Polonius swears he uses no art at all, and in fact what he does could hardly pass for artful oratory. It may be the truth as Polonius sees it (one has met such people who are simply unaware of how they circle a subject), or it may be false modesty (Polonius complacently pretending he does not know he is embellishing, or as he thinks, adorning, his thoughts).

> I have a daughter (have while she is mine),
> Who in her duty and obedience, mark,
> Hath given me this.
> (106–8)

Hamlet's love letter contains fairly conventional lover's compliments and does not tell us whether as much passion is in-

volved as Polonius wishes to find there. Polonius's tale of
quizzing his daughter, discovering Hamlet's love, forbidding
her to speak to him or receive his messages, and the results
which he has perceived or imagined, is Shakespeare's common
device of a review of action we have heard described by others
or seen for ourselves. The review always tells us more about
the speaker than about the events recounted; Claudius's account at 1.2.17–25 of the Fortinbras threat (about which we
have already heard in 1.1) is an example. The last part of this
account of Hamlet is conned from received wisdom about the
pining lover; at this moment Polonius appears less a man of
observation or experience than one whose advice and wit
comes from memorization of the standard sources:

> And he, repellèd, a short tale to make,
> Fell into a sadness, then into a fast,
> Thence to a watch, thence into a weakness,
> Thence to a lightness, and, by this declension,
> Into the madness wherein now he raves.
>
> (146–50)

Claudius's and Gertrude's provisional acceptance of this account is probably no more than a hope each has, for different
reasons. Claudius wants to "try it further" (159) on account of
his own fear or his distrust of Polonius's explanation. When
Polonius asks the king whether his chief counselor has ever
been wrong when he positively said a thing was so (and Polonius's being so straightforward as to say a thing was so, without qualification, is difficult to imagine), Claudius answers
equivocally, "Not that I know" (155).

Polonius's spying plan is his second and penultimate:

> You know sometimes he walks four hours together
> Here in the lobby. . . .
> At such a time I'll loose my daughter to him.
> Be you and I behind an arras then.
> Mark the encounter.
>
> (160–64)

Hamlet's entry is directed after the king's line "We will try it" in
both the Quarto and Folio texts. Nevertheless, Dover Wilson

has argued that Polonius's line 160–61 above "is equivalent to a stage-direction, and marks with practical certainty the moment at which Hamlet comes in and the place of his entry" (107)— the place being the inner stage (Wilson adopts the Adams model for the Globe). The evidence for Hamlet's early entry, according to Wilson, is the way he talks to Polonius, calling him a fishmonger and using other expressions that can be glossed as referring to prostitution and pandering. All of this proves for Wilson that Hamlet heard Polonius speak of "loosing" his daughter to Hamlet and understood the word to mean "let her go for his carnal use" (103). If Wilson's argument is admitted, it is too easy to extend. When, for instance, Hamlet asks Polonius the question, to which he knows well enough the answer, "Have you a daughter?" (182) one could argue that he mockingly echoes Polonius's silly and self-evident figure at 106, "I have a daughter (have while she is mine)." Moreover, later in the scene, Hamlet's telling Rosencrantz and Guildenstern they were sent for, and telling them why, could be seen as evidence that he has been eavesdropping since the beginning of the scene.

What is the point of such speculation? Well, we may genuinely have some textual ambiguity in addition to that written into the play's lines, and it makes a difference to our view of Hamlet. Dover Wilson cannot stand the idea of a Hamlet who would deliberately eavesdrop on the king: "It would never do, for example, to let him linger in his place of concealment," Wilson says, because the audience might "suspect him of deliberate spying" (107). But a Hamlet who becomes as petty and intriguing as Polonius is not beyond our range of possibilities for the character.

The Prince's Interviews

Hamlet's conversation with Polonius has been much glossed and annotated; we know Hamlet is mocking Polonius, though there are disagreements about exactly how:

POLONIUS. Do you know me, my lord?

HAMLET. Excellent well. You are a fishmonger.

POLONIUS. Not I, my lord.

HAMLET. Then I would you were so honest a man.

POLONIUS. Honest, my lord?

HAMLET. Ay, sir. To be honest, as this world goes, is to be
   one man picked out of ten thousand.

POLONIUS. That's very true, my lord.

HAMLET. For if the sun breed maggots in a dead dog, being
   a good kissing carrion—Have you a daughter?

POLONIUS. I have, my lord.

HAMLET. Let her not walk i' th' sun. Conception is a
   blessing, but as your daughter may conceive, friend,
   look to 't.

(173–85)

Hamlet calls Polonius a fishmonger, which ought to be insulting regardless in what sense it is taken, and he begins to talk
about honesty, breeding, and conception. *Honest* and *honesty*
are almost as important in this play as William Empson has
shown them to be in *Othello* (218–49). Hamlet uses the words
half a dozen times in this scene and half a dozen more in the
next, where we shall have occasion to look at his concern with
honesty again. The Hamlet who puts special stress on honesty
here is the priggish one—he would bowdlerize Juvenal (line
200) and keep daughters locked up lest they seem to conceive
spontaneously, by themselves.

Spoken to a second time by Polonius, Hamlet turns his reference from Ophelia to Polonius himself:

the satirical rogue says here that old men have grey beards,
that their faces are wrinkled, their eyes purging thick amber
and plum-tree gum, and that they have a plentiful lack of
wit, together with most weak hams. All which, sir, though
I most powerfully and potently believe, yet I hold it not
honesty to have it thus set down, for you yourself, sir,
should be old as I am if, like a crab, you could go backward.

(195–202)

Warburton was the first to suggest that Hamlet is reading the
tenth satire of Juvenal (Furness 151). Juvenal's description of
the effects of age is capped by an explicit passage depicting in

clinical detail the loss of virility in an old man (lines 204–9).
Juvenal, says Hamlet, is not being honest (honorable, respect-
able, decorous) by being too honest (truthful) in this passage—
or the effect is not honest (chaste). All of these senses of the
word may be employed in "I would you were so honest a
man" above. Hamlet gives Polonius a fair chance to see that he
is not crazy and a reasonably explicit warning to keep himself
and Ophelia out of the way, although it may be argued that
Hamlet knows from the reception of his first words that Polonius is not going to take anything he says seriously. The range
of these speeches is tremendously wide. Hamlet can be playing with Polonius in the broadest possible way, taking advantage of the comic potential of the scene; as Dr. Johnson said,
"The pretended madness of Hamlet causes much mirth" (196).
He can also be very grim.

Rosencrantz and Guildenstern enter at 216, and their greeting concerns the "strumpet" Fortune (they introduce her and
Hamlet reminds them she is a strumpet) and whether the
world has grown honest—Hamlet thinks not. The priggish
Hamlet can emphasize these lines with distaste; the playful
Hamlet nudges his schoolfellows and boisterously turns the
conversation to "country matters":

> GUILDENSTERN. On Fortune's cap we are not the very
> button.
> HAMLET. Nor the soles of her shoe?
> ROSENCRANTZ. Neither, my lord.
> HAMLET. Then you live about her waist, or in the middle of
> her favors?
>
> (226–30)

The conversation introduces a theme picked up in subsequent
lines, since our position in regard to Fortune and our attitude
toward our place there makes the distinction between humility
and ambition. Hamlet immediately begins to question Rosencrantz and Guildenstern about their presence in Denmark. He
calls it a prison (239), which allows them to put off his question
by talking about why he thinks it so:

ROSENCRANTZ. Why, then your ambition makes it one. 'Tis
   too narrow for your mind.
HAMLET. O God, I could be bounded in a nutshell and
   count myself a king of infinite space, were it not that I
   have bad dreams.
GUILDENSTERN. Which dreams indeed are ambition, for
   the very substance of the ambitious is merely the
   shadow of a dream.
HAMLET. A dream itself is but a shadow.
ROSENCRANTZ. Truly, and I hold ambition of so airy and
   light a quality that it is but a shadow's shadow.
                                                (249–59)

Salvador de Madariaga argues that it is only natural for Rosencrantz and Guildenstern, knowing nothing of King Hamlet's
murder, to suppose that Hamlet's problem is frustrated ambition. Madariaga goes farther to say that his problem *is* at least
partly that (15). Most stage interpretations, however, have
Rosencrantz and Guildenstern protesting too much, assuming
their own motives drive everyone. Hamlet returns to his topic,
and presses them to admit they were sent for (285). At this
point Rosencrantz's question "What say you?" is often played
as an aside, or whispered, as in Maurice Evans's production
(Evans 93). Michael Taylor reminds us that none of the original
texts directs that this speech should be an aside: "Such a question could be frank, straight-forward, and manly—even and
direct—were it asked with no concern for Hamlet's listening
presence" (647). Taylor's point is that we too easily accept
Hamlet's characterization of these two as the only truth (648–
49). Taylor thinks we should have productions that show their
"true, bewildered, dignified selves" (652).
    There follows a set speech of Hamlet's that begins with a
denial of what they have come to discover: he says he does not
know why he has changed. Hamlet gives a fair description of
melancholy and then the paean to man, compounded, as Theodore Spencer has shown, of those ideas reverently set forth in
La Primaudaye and irreverently attacked by Montaigne (Spencer 3–4, 100). The speech may even owe something to the cho-

rus in *Antigone*. For our purposes the question is not the source
of the speech but how it may be spoken. The very phrases and
punctuation of this speech might be considered a paradigm of
the ambiguities of *Hamlet*. The Second Quarto has it thus:

> What peece of worke is a man, how noble in reason, how
> infinit in faculties, in forme and moouing, how expresse
> and admirable in action, how like an Angell in appre-
> hension, how like a God: the beautie of the world . . .

The Folio has it thus:

> What a piece of worke is a man! how Noble in Reason? how
> infinite in faculty? in forme and mouing how expresse and
> admirable? in Action, how like an Angell? in apprehension,
> how like a God the beauty of the world . . .

The logic of the passage strikes many people as self-evident,
but for some people it is the logic of the Quarto (why compare
man to an angel in *action*, since it must be in matters of spirit
that he is like angels?), while for others it is the logic of the
Folio (consider the parallelism and rise of *in action how like an
angel, in apprehension how like a God*). It is significant, I think,
that such modern editors as Dover Wilson, Willard Farnham,
Cyrus Hoy, T. J. B. Spencer, and Edward Hubler, all using the
Second Quarto as the primary text, split over this reading.
Wilson and Hoy go for a modified version of the Quarto punctuation, Farnham, Spencer and Hubler for a modified version
of the Folio reading. Perhaps Harold Jenkins's Arden Shakespeare *Hamlet* illustrates best the way such cruxes are resolved:
after pointing out that the "higher authority is with Q2 as believed printed from Shakespeare's autograph, and F's handling
of the punctuation in general entitles it to little weight" (468–
69), Jenkins nevertheless adopts the Folio reading. He offers as
evidence the "rhythmic imbalance" of the other reading, the
observation that this reading is "more in line with Hamlet's
way of thought," and an apparent parallel of the passage in
Marston's *Malcontent* (469–70).

The ambiguity extends beyond the grouping of phrases to
tone. Is the speech earnest? Rosencrantz cannot keep a straight

face at the speech, and it may be that his stated reason for
smiling or laughing (Hamlet's use of both words gives us a
range of possible reactions on Rosencrantz's part) is the simple
truth. Actors want to play Hamlet's speech as straight, and it
very often is so played. But Rosencrantz can just as likely be
reacting to a Hamlet who is unconsciously or consciously parodying the melancholy young man.

Hamlet may be consciously overacting the speech to
provoke a laugh from Rosencrantz—and then jumping on the
very reaction he has provoked. This reading fits a pattern of
Hamlet's treatment of Rosencrantz and Guildenstern evident
as the scene and the play progresses. Within the scene Hamlet
goes from cordial greeting to impatient questioning:

> GUILDENSTERN. What should we say, my lord?
> HAMLET. Why, anything—but to th' purpose.
> (274–75)

Before the scene ends, Hamlet excuses his neglect of them
(when he turns his attention to the players) and ceremoniously
takes their hands, saying that the "appurtenance of welcome is
fashion and ceremony" (362); two scenes later he will be suggesting that their inability to play a simple instrument ("It is as
easy as lying" 3.2.343) ought to instruct them how to stay away
from more complex ones. Later he calls them sponges and
fools (4.2.15–23). Hamlet begins by greeting his "excellent
good friends" warmly; he ends with a conscience untouched
by having sent them to their deaths.

Whatever provokes Rosencrantz's smiling or laughing, at
Hamlet's question about it the topic turns to the players.
Hamlet's very quick response (314–20) promises more than
"lenten entertainment" for each of them; perhaps he is merely
cheered by the prospect of a diversion which has been his special delight in the past. But he begins with a significant player:

> He that plays the king shall be welcome—his majesty shall
> have tribute of me.
> (314–15)

The choice indicates that Hamlet has an immediate thought of the players as a way of saying what he cannot or dare not say himself to the king.

A twenty-five-line discussion follows in the First Folio concerning the rivalry between the children's companies and the adult players. It is not in the Second Quarto, but there is enough indication of it in the First Quarto (lines 974–77) to assure us that it was part of the play in its first years. The topical nature of the passage overshadows its thematic significance in describing another conflict of youth and age, another wrongful and (as Hamlet explains, when he points out at line 344 that the children "exclaim against their own succession") unnatural usurpation. Everything to do with the players has thematic importance in a play so concerned with acting, playing, and seeming, a play in which, as Maynard Mack has written, "the most pervasive of Shakespeare's image patterns" is that using the words *show, act,* and *play,* with *show* the "unifying image" and *act* the "radical metaphor" (Mack 512–13). Of course Hamlet makes a direct application of the children's company's new popularity to the main matter of the play:

> It is not very strange, for my uncle is King of Denmark, and those that would make mows at him while my father lived give twenty, forty, fifty, a hundred ducats apiece for his picture in little. (355–58)

In Maurice Evans's production Hamlet reaches for a medallion pinned to the lapel of Rosencrantz's coat at the last line. He follows this speech, which ought to give his friends a clear idea of his feeling about Claudius, with a repetition of their welcome and an apology for any appearance of greater welcome to the players.

> HAMLET. You are welcome. But my uncle-father and aunt-mother are deceived.
> GUILDENSTERN. In what, my dear lord?
> HAMLET. I am but mad north-north-west. When the wind is southerly I know a hawk from a handsaw.
> (366–70)

With his "uncle-father" and "aunt-mother" Hamlet underlines
what he takes to be the unnatural relationship he bears Gertrude and Claudius, as they bear each other. Compare:

> I am too much in the sun
> (1.2.67)

> We shall obey, were she ten times our mother
> (3.2.319)

> [to Claudius] Farewell, dear mother
> (4.3.48)

Rosencrantz and Guildenstern have been warned that Hamlet
is not mad, though the warning is equivocal, since the mad are
likely to deny their condition. Hamlet may play this line with a
lunatic air or even—almost as negating—a conspiratorial one.

When Polonius comes to introduce the actors, Hamlet toys
with him in what is at once low comedy and still on the serious
subject of his daughter and her uses.

> POLONIUS. The actors are come hither, my lord.
> HAMLET. Buzz, buzz.
> POLONIUS. Upon my honor—
> HAMLET. Then came each actor on his ass—
> (383–86)

Hamlet's unmistakable raspberry finally gets some reaction
from Polonius, whose thoughts are frequently on his honor.
But when Hamlet calls Polonius's honor an ass, Polonius can
choose to ignore it, as he can ignore also the implications of
Hamlet's identifying him with Jephthah, who sacrificed his
daughter to fulfill a rash promise he had made to his god-king.
Another possibility is that some more noticeable friction begins
to develop between the two men here, lending sharpness to
Hamlet's taunts before the play in 3.2, Polonius's words to
Gertrude in 3.4 that Hamlet's "pranks have been too broad to
bear with," and Hamlet's rough reaction to discovering that he
has killed Polonius later in the same scene.

The players enter at 410. Hamlet knows and greets several
of them individually. He wants a small performance on the

spot, and not surprisingly, he tells them what speech and begins it himself. Wherever else Hamlet may be merely "instrument rather than agent" (Johnson 196), during this scene and throughout Act Three he controls events. He baits Polonius, preempts the interrogation by Rosencrantz and Guildenstern, begins an impromptu performance by the players and plans a more elaborate one, writing his own speech for it. He coaches the players, enlists Horatio's aid in watching Claudius, acts as a chorus to the play, sees the king's reaction to it, chooses not to kill him at prayer, lashes his mother's conscience, and kills Polonius.

Almost a hundred lines of this scene are devoted to the "rugged Pyrrhus" speech, introduced and begun by Hamlet, then continued by the player. Hamlet asks for a passionate speech, from a play that was not popular, but good.

> 'Twas Aeneas' tale to Dido, and thereabout of it especially
> where he speaks of Priam's slaughter. (434–36)

The subject matter of the speech is the death of a father, Priam. Moreover, what we might call the frame story of the speech, the tale of Aeneas, is the story of a loved father and a dutiful son. Priam is an archetypal father in the sense that he is the chief father in the archetypal story of Troy and its fall, and also in the sense that he has fathered so many children and especially, fifty sons. Then too, the story is one of a son's revenge, since Pyrrhus was the son of Achilles, though his vengeance is exacted not on Paris, who actually killed his father, but on Paris's father Priam, Priam's youngest son Polites, and others.

That Hamlet is capable of rapping out a dozen lines of blank verse tells something of how much delight he was "wont to take" in the players and their craft; that he picks this particular speech tells more significantly that he is approaching the murder of his father obliquely. His part of the speech describes Pyrrhus, in his black armor; it is the killer rather than the wronged victim who is armed from top to toe in this tale. Pyrrhus's armor is covered with "blood of fathers, mothers, daughters, sons" (446)—emblems of a more general slaughter than the murder of one father. Hamlet's approach to the real topic on his mind need not be conscious or deliberate; he does not have to know himself how Priam's slaughter came to be dredged up from memory. But he does have the players play "something like the murther" of his father *twice*, in two successive acts, the second representation being the closer one. And though the second performance is designed to provoke a reaction in Claudius, both these shows are also cues to passion for Hamlet himself. From one point of view they may be seen as attempts to assimilate the reality of his father's murder, which Hamlet can only look at whole after he has seen a denatured, classical version. From another point of view we may be looking at a Hamlet who calls for these shows, not in order to come to terms with the past, but in order to charge himself for action in the future.

The description of the actual murder Hamlet leaves to the player. Pyrrhus's sword falls at 480, and the reaction (presumably from the filial Aeneas, recalling all this) is: "Out, out, thou strumpet Fortune!" (481). Nor is this the only iteration of earlier remarks about Fortune, for we are told that had we seen Hecuba at this moment, we would have pronounced treason "'Gainst Fortune's state" (499). It is to Hecuba that the player turns next, at Hamlet's request: the fatherless son is naturally interested in how the mother takes her husband's death. The subject now is a motive for passion:

> But if the gods themselves did see her then,
> When she saw Pyrrhus make malicious sport
> In mincing with his sword her husband's limbs,
> The instant burst of clamor that she made
> (Unless things mortal move them not at all)
> Would have made milch the burning eyes of heaven
> And passion in the gods.
>
> (500–506)

But it is passion in the player which affects Polonius and Hamlet, and to which Hamlet will return as soon as he is alone. First he dismisses the players, to the keeping of Polonius, whom he instructs to use them, not according to their deserving, but better: "Use every man after his desert, and who shall scape whipping? Use them after your own honor and dignity" (516–17). As aimed strictly at Polonius, who suspects even those nearest to him of offenses that might merit whipping, Hamlet's remark is apt. But he is not necessarily just playing to Polonius. Hamlet shows us a range of response to human potential from a Renaissance ideal of man as the beauty of the world and paragon of animals to a Calvinist view of him as depraved, "crawling between earth and heaven" (3.1.128). It may be too simple to say, as Theodore Spencer and Maynard Mack do in so many words, that Hamlet begins with the one and, through disillusionment, is plunged into the other. Different productions emphasize different places on this scale; Olivier's film, for example, shows the Prince as a consistent Puritan, Richardson's Hamlet reacts to the world's depravity with anger and bad manners, Kozintsev's Prince discovers political and philosophical truths with a serious rather than surprised or melancholy demeanor, and Derek Jacobi's Hamlet seems to have had a sophomore's cynicism about human ideals even before he encounters the nasty revelations of the play.

In the few moments between the end of the player's speech and the beginning of his soliloquy, Hamlet is busy. Such juxtapositions make *Hamlet* a play of paradoxes: just before Hamlet proceeds to chastise himself for being dull, cowardly, and inactive, he has been at his most active, clear-headed, charitable, quick-thinking, and decisive—charging Polonius to care for the players according to his own honor and dignity, taking the chief player aside and planning for the morrow a play which he knows to be like his father's murder (if the ghost was telling the truth) and which he will make more so by the addition of his own speech, instructing the player not to make fun of Polonius, and reiterating his welcome to Rosencrantz and Guildenstern.

At 533 he is alone. His soliloquy here is the longest (57 lines) in the play. Hamlet's judgments of himself here are, like his critiques of others, extreme and absolute. When he assesses himself as pigeon-livered, dull, and muddy-mettled, the very presentation (in a decisive Hamlet) as well as the surrounding circumstances will work to remind us of his clarity of mind, his courage and resolution, and those qualities that he denies here. A weaker reading of the speech will take emphasis away from any appearance of decisiveness in the preceding action and show us a Hamlet closer to the one that Hamlet himself sees when he looks inward.

The Hamlet who values himself at a worse rate than he deserves is still telling the truth according to the conventions of soliloquy. What he calls himself is not necessarily what we perceive; even though it is a true soul-baring and genuinely the character's view of the world and of himself, it need not correspond to our view. A. J. A. Waldock thinks Hamlet stronger than the portrait he paints of himself here: "Are we really made to feel, by the speech, that it is strange that Hamlet has not yet acted? Do we concur in his wonder at himself and join with him in his self-reproaches? A Shakespearean soliloquy is often naive; but surely not quite so naive as that" (86). Hamlet begins by calling it monstrous that the player can get into such a passion over a fiction. He asks what the player would do if he had Hamlet's reasons, and answers that he would be in a great passion. Then, as if he suddenly recalls that the point is not working up a passion, but doing something about it, Hamlet calls himself pigeon livered for not killing Claudius earlier. He curses Claudius and then reviles himself for cursing "like a very drab" (572). This Hamlet will probably put more emphasis on the trap he is laying for Claudius, which is dealt with in lines 575 to the end of the soliloquy.

A Hamlet closer to the "soul unfit" of Goethe and Coleridge will stress doubt about the ghost's honesty (584–89) as an excuse for inaction. He will emphasize the line that mentions his "weakness" and "melancholy" (587) and play up the outburst and loss of control in the middle of the soliloquy:

> Bloody, bawdy villain!
> Remorseless, treacherous, lecherous, kindless villain!
> O, vengeance!

> Why, what an ass am I! This is most brave,
> That I, the son of a dear father murthered,
> Prompted to my revenge by heaven and hell,
> Must like a whore unpack my heart with words
> And fall a-cursing like a very drab,
> A stallion! Fie upon't, foh! About, my brains.
> Hum—
>
> (565–74)

Olivier took the most drastic approach: he cut the entire soliloquy except for the last line and a half. But then, he had already loaded the audience response to one side by announcing at the beginning of his film, "This is the tragedy of a man who could not make up his mind."

Act Three

Each of the next four scenes is a play scene, with spectacle and onstage audience, making explicit a rhythm of action that has been less noticeably present since the beginning of the play. In each, one or more spectators watch silently at the periphery of an action while one or more persons at the center speak and act. The audience arrives, the show is played out, the audience reacts and departs. Polonius arranges the first and last of these scenes, both spy scenes in which one of the two people spied on is a woman who knows of the arrangement, and the other person is Hamlet, who does not know of it. Hamlet arranges the middle two scenes, since he chooses the text of the play within the play and even writes some of it, he instructs the actors in its proper playing, and his stinging of the king's conscience is (we assume) the cause of Claudius's attempted repentance in 3.3.

In each scene there is really only one important onstage spectator: the king in 3.1 and 3.2, Hamlet in 3.3, and Polonius as long as he is alive in 3.4. But the most important onstage reactions are those of Claudius and Hamlet. Claudius's first lash of conscience comes as the first little playlet is being set up by Polonius in 3.1; his more extensive attack of guilt comes after the play within the play in 3.2. Claudius reacts to the play by deciding to send Hamlet to England; he reacts to the closet scene by deciding to have him killed there. The play within the play has of course been set up to provoke a reaction in Claudius, and it does. Hamlet reacts to the play by becoming convinced that his revenge is now justified; he reacts to Claudius at prayer by postponing that revenge. The scenes demonstrate that watching is as various as playing, and an art of watching is implied by the fact that Hamlet instructs Horatio—his audience—as well as the players. Spectating may be open or clandestine, "lawful espials" or unnecessary and unseemly spying. It may be amusement or mortal danger. Spectators may learn the truth from a true or nearly true representation (3.2), they may learn the truth from a partly false representation (3.1), they may mistake a true representation and thus learn a falsehood from it (3.3), or they may learn nothing, except that "to be too busy is some danger" (3.4.34).

Scene One

This scene begins and ends with the king talking of the danger of Hamlet's state of mind. The emotional temperature has gone up from the previous scene, which began with Claudius asking Rosencrantz and Guildenstern to find some pleasant activities for Hamlet and to find out what is wrong with him—"Whether aught to us unknown afflicts him thus, That opened lies within our remedy" (2.2.17–18). The king has just been told of the failure of Rosencrantz and Guildenstern's mission to discover from Hamlet, in Claudius's words, "why he puts on this confusion" (2). The Machiavellian Claudius has already let slip the mask of kindly concern; underneath we glimpse the strong suspicion that Hamlet is faking. Claudius is not even hiding his concern that Hamlet's condition is dangerous.

> There's something in his soul
> O'er which his melancholy sits on brood,
> And I do doubt the hatch and the disclose
> Will be some danger.
>
> (3.1. 164–67)

The Machiavellian Claudius can easily convey that he does not mean "danger" to Hamlet, but to himself, and that it is time to begin thinking of what must be done to control the prince or destroy him. But another Claudius is less sure of himself here, trapped between his desire for safety and his awareness of Gertrude's love for her son. Claudius ultimately finds himself impaled on the horns of dilemmas concerning all three of the revengers, Hamlet, Laertes, and Fortinbras. All threaten his security. To defuse Fortinbras's threat, Claudius must accede to Norway's demand of a free pass for Fortinbras's armies, and Fortinbras's free passage will ultimately allow him to walk onto Denmark's throne. To keep Laertes from threatening his person and his crown, Claudius will have to arrange Hamlet's death. To kill Hamlet, Claudius will have to hurt and finally kill Gertrude. Although he knows none of this now, Claudius may by his demeanor convey a lack of control, the "hugger-mugger" he will speak of in Act Four, desperately concealed. When this Claudius is attacked by his conscience, as he is shortly to be, he shows us a man less tortured by his concealed moral nature than appalled by chaos opening beneath him. The stronger Claudius may convince us of a real moral sense suppressed, but this one will not.

At the scene's beginning, Rosencrantz and Guildenstern give a not completely accurate report of their interview with Hamlet. We can confirm that Hamlet confessed himself distracted without saying why, that he was not "forward to be sounded" (7), and that he was pleased with the players' arrival. Their assessment of his being "Niggard of question, but of our demands / Most free in his reply" (13–14) is less than candid. As Tom Stoppard has Rosencrantz say in *Rosencrantz and Guildenstern Are Dead:*

> It was question and answer, all right. Twenty-seven questions he got out in ten minutes, and answered three. . . .
> Six rhetorical and two repetition, leaving nineteen, of which we answered fifteen. And what did we get in return? He's depressed! . . . Denmark's a prison and he'd rather live in a nutshell; some shadow-play about the nature of ambition, which never got down to cases, and finally one direct question which might have led somewhere, and led in fact to his illuminating claim to tell a hawk from a handsaw.
>
> (57)

Rosencrantz and Guildenstern do not report Hamlet's remark about his uncle-father and aunt-mother being deceived—that he is mad merely north-northwest. It is possible to see the two of them concealing these aspects of their interview through concern for Hamlet. Productions usually give us oily versions of these two characters, but there are other possibilities, as defined by Hamlet's own words. They may in fact be his "excellent good friends" (2.2.222), whatever words they give the king. They may be pure creatures of ambition, who "make love to this employment" (5.2.57). Stoppard's characters are men who have some affection for Hamlet, have some ambition as well, but are mainly people caught "Between the pass and fell incensèd points / Of mighty opposites" (5.2.61–62), in Hamlet's words; in their own words they are "the indifferent children of the earth" (2.2.224), and, we may add, children among dangerous adults.

At least one part of their news is pleasing: Hamlet has been diverted by the players, who will present a play before the whole company that night. Rosencrantz and Guildenstern exit. Claudius repeats to Gertrude the plan to spy on Hamlet:

> And gather by him, as he is behaved,
> If't be th' affliction of his love or no
> That thus he suffers for.
>
> (35–37)

Gertrude tells Ophelia that she hopes the girl is "the happy cause / Of Hamlet's wildness" and that she may also be the cure. The speech seems ingenuous, and is confirmed by what Gertrude says much later, over Ophelia's grave, about the hope that she and Hamlet might have married. Gertrude must wish Ophelia the cause of Hamlet's state of mind, since the only alternatives she could envision would be worse: either the main cause, as she has called it, "his father's death and our o'erhasty marriage" (2.2.57), or, if we grant her further guilt, his father's murder and his mother's adultery. But if Gertrude knows of these things she has given no sign. It is in character for a certain kind of Gertrude to hope that love will solve all problems; this is not the same Queen who advises Claudius about tactical matters and values him for his decisiveness, even his ruthlessness, though she cannot wish the latter quality turned on her son, as it will be.

Polonius sets up the encounter between Ophelia and Hamlet, who has been "closely sent for": he instructs Ophelia where to walk and gives her a devotional book to read. His comment, that "with devotion's visage / And pious action we do sugar o'er / The devil himself" (47–49), provokes Claudius's first show of conscience:

> KING.   [aside] O 'tis too true.
> How smart a lash that speech doth give my conscience!
> The harlot's cheek, beautied with plast'ring art,
> Is not more ugly to the thing that helps it
> Than is my deed to my most painted word.
> O heavy burthen!
>
>   (49–54)

The speech looks backward and forward in the play. Its testimony of the most important witness confirms for us (in case we have any of the same doubts expressed by Hamlet fifty lines earlier) that Claudius is guilty. By making us realize that until this moment we were not *sure* of Claudius's guilt the speech vindicates those doubts of Hamlet. The strong Claudius has given no indication of shame or guilt to this point. The weak Claudius or the drunkard have been too easy for us to detest as much as Hamlet does and therefore to condemn out of hand. But this small confession, provoked by Polonius's little play, is also a forecast of Claudius's more complete confession later, after Hamlet's play.

Hamlet's entry and his most famous soliloquy come at line 56. The "To be or not to be" soliloquy has always been more popular than clear. One thing we should remember, as Harley Granville-Barker reminds us, is how little time has passed since Hamlet was decisively planning his trap for the king: "Before his last quiet entrance, reading on a book, we had heard of him distractedly intruding upon Ophelia. But a few moments since we have seen him equally torn with emotion; and here he is, outwardly calm and self-contained as never before" (77). Granville-Barker calls the shift in emotional tone

one of the typical contrasts of the play. In effect, the speech is very much of the chameleon's nature and takes easily the coloration of the particular Hamlet who speaks it. The speech can bear the emphasis of many Hamlets.

To begin at the lower end, it can bear the emphasis of a man who is too cowardly to act, who thinks of suicide as a way of relieving himself of the task before him, who then reveals himself too cowardly to commit suicide for fear of what might happen after death, and who finally generalizes his cowardice to all men (83–88). The speech will also accommodate a second Hamlet, unable to act because of psychological inhibitions which are not conscious (Jones 59), because of melancholy (Bradley 104–9), because of excessive grief or "melancholy adust" (Campbell 110), or because of some other psychological restraint such as "a soul unfit for the performance" of a great action (Goethe 282). This Hamlet is attempting to explain to himself why he is not acting, beginning with an extension of remarks about suicide he made in his first soliloquy. It may be somewhat difficult for an actor to make the distinction here between words impelled by melancholy and those forced from him by melancholy adust, but he may be assured that the learned critic in the audience will be able to discriminate and applaud the difference.

The speech will be read quite differently by those Hamlets who have not yet accomplished their revenge because of considerations other than psychological restraints. These men are up to the task before them, but are impeded by physical or ethical fears. One of them is the Hamlet who fears death—not out of cowardice, but because he feels his revenge on Claudius will be answered by his own death at the hands of Claudius's followers, who will think Hamlet merely treasonous so long as he cannot convict Claudius with anything more than his own account of the ghost's story (Werder 41–54). Other Hamlets are held back by moral scruples: one because he has not yet tested the ghost's story, as he has just recently told us (2.2.584–89); another because he has reservations about revenge itself. This last Hamlet is very close with his ethical doubts, though: he has never explicitly mentioned them, nor will he throughout the rest of the play. Nevertheless, he is a difficult Hamlet to dismiss for anyone who is used to Christian prohibitions against vengeance. He appealed to as sensitive a reader as George Santayana, and he finds his most cogent modern defender in Eleanor Prosser (Santayana 215–16; Harbage 98; Prosser 155–71).

All these more resolute Hamlets come together as one in the reading of this speech. Hamlet begins with the question whether it is better to bear one's fortune or to be dead, and most of the speech is about being dead. As C. S. Lewis pointed out in his Academy Lecture, in *Hamlet* we are kept thinking about being dead much of the time (13). But Hamlet is not speaking of suicide: "to take arms against a sea of troubles / And by opposing end them" means some more active and outward struggle which results in death. By line 75 it *is* clear that suicide is meant, but up to that point Hamlet is talking, in his own case, of death as the inevitable result of his taking public revenge on Claudius now. Yet he couches the whole in general terms: "*we* end / The heartache . . . When *we* have shuffled off this mortal coil" (61–62, 67) and so on.

These resolute Hamlets begin with questions about whether they ought to act in such a way as to cause their own deaths, move to what might happen after such deaths, and then, further generalizing, they go on to point out that if it were not for such fears, many who suffer would end their sufferings by suicide. The concluding six lines of the speech appear to be the same kind of chastisement for inaction that we saw in the concluding soliloquy of Act Two, but it is perhaps significant that they are couched in general terms. Hamlet speaks of the coward in all of us rather than calling himself pigeon-livered. Johnson says in concluding his remarks on this soliloquy, "We may suppose that he would have applied these general observations to his own case, but that he discovered Ophelia" (192).

The discovery of Ophelia reminds us that Hamlet has not been alone during his speech, and raises the question whether any of it was meant to be overheard. Hamlet may speak the lines in which he acknowledges Ophelia's presence with genuine or feigned surprise, and "Nymph, in thy orisons / Be all my sins remembered" (89–90) may be whispered sincerely or spoken aloud in anything from gentle to mocking tones. How much does Hamlet know of the "lawful espials" and when does he know it? Does Hamlet love Ophelia and how much does he show it, willingly or unwillingly? These are some of the questions whose answers govern the playing of the scene.

In the most venerable stage tradition, Hamlet discovers the presence of the king and Polonius by an inadvertent signal from Ophelia, by a noise, or by a glimpse of Polonius and Claudius up in the gallery—the last being Edwin Booth's way of playing the scene (Shattuck 190). The discovery comes usually just before Hamlet's question, "Where's your father?" (130) Thus, for example, in the BBC Shakespeare Plays *Hamlet*, the discovery is forecast at the first encounter of Hamlet and Ophelia: Derek Jacobi looks at Lalla Ward's book, turns it (she has been holding it upside down), and speaks the line about remembering him in her prayers. Then at "Why wouldst thou be a breeder of sinners?" (121) he reaches for her crotch; she evades him and glances at the doors behind which Patrick Stewart and Eric Porter listen. In Maurice Evans's version, Evans is kneeling in front of Janet Slauson at "Go thy ways to a nunnery" (129). She is about to caress his hair when she remembers the observers and looks toward the door. He sees her glance and asks, "Where's your father?" (Evans 110).

Dover Wilson's 1935 *What Happens in Hamlet* started a new tradition; Wilson argued that Hamlet inadvertently overheard Polonius setting up the spy scene when he entered an inner recess of the stage in 2.2 at "sometimes he walks four hours together / Here in the lobby," seven lines before the stage direction for his entry, which for Wilson means his entry to the outer stage (Wilson 107). Thus Hamlet knows of the "lawful espials" as soon as he sees Ophelia by herself. John Gielgud's 1936 production adopted Dover Wilson's ideas. Laurence Olivier has it both ways in his film version (1948). He spies upon the royal party in 2.2 (Wilson would have been horrified, since his Hamlet is too noble for anything but inadvertent over-hearing) and thus knows of the plan. When he meets Ophelia alone later on, he glances through doorways and begins to approach the arras to check for eavesdroppers, but as Ophelia kneels at a prie-dieu he is momentarily distracted. Then, as she is about to pull from her bosom Hamlet's "remembrances," Jean Simmons looks toward the arras where Basil Sydney and Felix Aylmer are concealed, and Olivier follows the glance.

The Wilson approach leaves open the possibility that some or all of Hamlet's talk of death, suicide, and conscience is intended to be overheard. Hamlet, however, seems surprised to see Ophelia at the end of his speech, and his "Nymph, in thy orisons / Be all my sins remembered" is for Roy Walker the denial to Dover Wilson's theory and a demonstration that Hamlet does not know or suspect her complicity in the spying (59). But the line, Hamlet's first spoken words to Ophelia in the play, need not be given gently. The intent of this line, if not its tone, will shortly be countered by Hamlet's questioning of Ophelia's chastity. He will also say he loved her, and then that he did not love her. There is no warrant for Hamlet's feelings in the lines of this scene. He loves her, or he loves her not. But these by no means exhaust the possible variations:

Hamlet loves Ophelia and wishes to convey this to her while trying to convince his other watchers (whenever he becomes aware of them) that he is mad. He does not succeed in either purpose; Ophelia is unwilling or too dense to be drawn into a conspiracy with him against her father and Claudius. When she attempts to return his "remembrances," he says "I never gave you aught"(96)—it was another Hamlet, not this one; this is a show. "I did love you once" (115) is whispered, but Ophelia comes back in full voice, and so Hamlet responds also in full voice to contradict what he had said. The accusations of painting, primping, and so on are thrown out because any one looking at Ophelia would see they were false and Hamlet mad to make them.

Hamlet loves Ophelia and successfully conveys this to her, however he may fare in his attempt to convince the others he is mad. Ophelia becomes Hamlet's accomplice in this deception; when Hamlet makes his remarks about her father she realizes he knows exactly what is going on and begins to respond to his acted madness: "O help him, you sweet heavens!" (134). She shows an unexpected talent for this sort of thing in her speech at his exit.

Hamlet loves Ophelia and cannot help the occasional indication of his love that escapes him although he is trying to play the scene for the sake of the others. His act involves contradictions, wide swings between shows of love and hate, but the sincerity of the love may peek through. Thus Jacobi's Hamlet bursts into tears about line 135 and speaks all the rest of the lines through them.

Hamlet is ambivalent about his feelings and alternately wishes to protect and to hurt Ophelia. Why might he desire to hurt Ophelia? He wishes to hurt her because he feels (rightly—Schucking, *Problems* 69—or wrongly—Walker 43–45) she has betrayed him and is of the court side, because he generalizes from his mother's behavior to include all women, seeing her as lustful and corrupt (Mack 521), or because of the latter reason at the unconscious level, that is, he is really punishing his mother in the person of Ophelia (Jones 83–99).

Hamlet may or may not love Ophelia, but in either case everything he does is directed solely at convincing the watchers he is mad.

Hamlet may or may not love Ophelia, but in either case his remarks about women are directed at the Queen, whom he believes to be listening. This suggestion comes from T. J. B. Spencer, in the notes to his New Penguin edition of the play. Spencer's thesis depends on Hamlet's believing Ophelia when she says her father is at home. He then concludes that the Queen must have brought Ophelia here and that she is eavesdropping (270).

Hamlet does not love Ophelia, and what he says is intended to hurt her as well as work on his other hearers. Thus when she attempts to return his letters (if that is what the "remembrances" are) he says "I never gave *you* aught"— that is, in Roy Walker's words, "His gifts were offered to his soul's idol, the Ophelia beautified from within, not to this scheming little bitch with the face of an angel" (59). In a subvariation of this view, Hamlet merely wants to hurt Ophelia, and does not care about or is completely unaware of the eavesdroppers. Hamlet's question about Ophelia's father, for example, may be motivated purely by what he feels to be her obsequiousness to Polonius rather than by his knowledge or suspicion of Polonius's presence.

Finally, Hamlet may or may not love Ophelia, but is simply mad.

Even the principal image in Hamlet's encounter with Ophelia, the nunnery of his repeated order to her (121, 129, 137, 140, 149), is an ambiguous one, since taken literally, it may represent protection from the world for the innocent or a punishment and removal from further temptation for the fallen, and it has the possible figurative meaning of a brothel. And the response to Hamlet's scene clarifies nothing, since Ophelia responds by thinking Hamlet mad (unless she is dissembling this reaction) while Claudius thinks what Hamlet said "Was not like madness" (164). W. S. Gilbert's Ophelia, in his *Rosencrantz and Guildenstern* (1891), has the best comment on the complexity of the situation here:

> Opinion is divided. Some men hold
> That he's the sanest far of all sane men—
> Some that he's really sane, but shamming mad—
> Some that he's really mad, but shamming sane—
> Some that he will be mad, some that he was—
> Some that he couldn't be. But on the whole
> (As far as I can make out what they mean)
> The favourite theory's somewhat like this:
> Hamlet is idiotically sane
> With lucid intervals of lunacy.
>
> (Gilbert 80)

Shakespeare's Ophelia laments the mind overthrown by madness, and her picture of Hamlet is one of the few glimpses we get of him as he was before his series of shocks (he himself gives us such a glimpse in his first talk with Rosencrantz and Guildenstern, and Fortinbras briefly tells us at the end of the play that Hamlet "was likely . . . to have proved most royal"—5.2.385–86). The speech tells us as much about Ophelia as about Hamlet:

> The courtier's, soldier's, scholar's, eye, tongue, sword,
> Th' expectancy and rose of the fair state,
> The glass of fashion and the mould of form,
> Th' observed of all observers, quite, quite down!
> And I, of ladies most deject and wretched,
> That sucked the honey of his music vows,
> Now see that noble and most sovereign reason
> Like sweet bells jangled, out of time and harsh,
> That unmatched form and feature of blown youth
> Blasted with ecstasy. O, woe is me
> T' have seen what I have seen, see what I see!
>
> (151–61)

Ophelia could possibly be speaking solely for the benefit of Polonius and Claudius. The portrait of Hamlet here may merely be a romantic ideal with which she has fallen in love, rather than the real Hamlet. But the speech is most remarkable, coming just before the middle scene of the play, contrasting past and present, ironically forecasting Ophelia's future. Its balanced and symmetrical pairings and antitheses show us the Ophelia as well as the Hamlet of the past and the present in language that belies any tunelessness or lack of keeping time: Hamlet *was* the expectancy and rose, the glass and mould of fashion and form; Ophelia *is* deject and wretched; Hamlet's noble and sovereign reason is out of time and harsh, his youth blasted in form and feature; all this Ophelia has seen in the past and does see now. She does not see how her reaction to this woe is a forecast of *her* madness, nor that she is less able to cope with the time's being out of joint than Hamlet.

If Hamlet was attempting to show that love was the cause of his madness he has failed. Polonius, indeed, still believes

"The origin and commencement of his grief / Sprung from ne-
glected love" (177–78), but Claudius is certain Hamlet is not in
love. Moreover, though Claudius at first says of Hamlet that
what he spoke "Was not like madness," he concludes the scene
by saying "Madness in great ones must not unwatched go"
(188). Hamlet has fooled Claudius only if his madness is real.
His pretended madness has not only failed to convince the
king; it has now become the king's tool to send Hamlet away.
And the belief of others that Hamlet is mad, for whatever reason, will only assist Claudius in ridding himself of the danger
he sees:

> There's something in his soul
> O'er which his melancholy sits on brood,
> And I do doubt the hatch and the disclose
> Will be some danger; which for to prevent,
> I have in quick determination
> Thus set it down: he shall with speed to England
>   (164–69)

Claudius apparently cannot yet justify to himself the killing of
Hamlet, but Polonius ironically prepares that justification by
setting up the last eavesdropping scene, which will lead to his
own death.

Scene Two

The Murder of Gonzago comes at the middle of Hamlet. In
most editions, the exact center of the play coincides with the
speaking of the brief prologue to the play within the play, and
of all Shakespeare's plays within plays, none is so central figur-
atively to its host play's action. Hamlet is not about the murder
of a king but about the revelation of that murder and what
happens as a result of the revelation, though much more about
the revelation itself, which is not even finished at the end of
the play. Hamlet is a play about playing with a play at its center.

The men and women at Elsinore play parts to conceal guilt or knowledge of guilt and to pry into secrets. They assume appearances to conceal reality. The actors of *The Murder of Gonzago* assume roles to reveal reality. The play within the play is that place where the whole fiction can be grasped and turned inside out, into truth.

The play within the play shows us a murder we could not otherwise see. We must get our report of the murder either from the dead, from the one living man who knows of it directly, the murderer, or else "in a fiction, a dream of passion." We get all three, but significantly, the fiction most vividly gives us the scene, in dumb show and in dialogue with action.

The little play also shows the murder to Hamlet and Claudius. In fact, both Hamlet and Claudius see the murder of old Hamlet for the first time as they watch the play within the play. For Hamlet, regardless of how we take his expressed doubts about the ghost at 2.2.584, regardless of whether he believes or does not believe the account of his father's death, regardless of whether he is trying to get on with his revenge or finding excuses for his delay, the little play and its results not only confirm the ghost's story but also, at least fleetingly, affect Hamlet as the real thing being played before him, as his excitement and his intervention at the critical moment show. Claudius, on the other hand, has participated in the scene being represented in the little play. He knows about it in conscience and memory, but he has not seen it. When he reacts as he does (and depending on the interpretation, we may not see his reaction, but only know of it by his words in the next scene) it may be not because he has discovered that Hamlet knows his secret but because he sees his deed for the first time as it really is.

Hamlet's Address to the Players

The play provides Hamlet with a chance to arrange experience, to give an order and meaning to portrayed events which the real thing lacks. Hamlet gives the players instructions about speaking (1–4), gesturing (4–5), tempering mood (5–8), and modeling their words and actions according to "the modesty of nature" (15–23). Hamlet argues for a natural style; he dislikes not only bad actors but mannered ones as well. He is concerned that the general performance be received as a realistic portrayal, but also that his own contribution not be obscured. When he directs that the clowns "speak no more than is set down for them" (37), for example, he wants to avoid laughter where it is not warranted and to keep the play from degenerating into farce. More specifically, he is concerned that extemporaneous clowning might obscure "some necessary question of the play" (40). He wants "the very cunning of the scene" (2.2.576), unimpeded by mannered acting or slapstick, to strike Claudius to the soul.

How the players receive Hamlet's advice is a question left fairly open by the text. We may look to specific interpretations to define the range here. Olivier's players obediently accept all that the master actor has instructed them to do. Less obsequiously, Emrys James, the First Player in the BBC television *Hamlet*, follows a busybody Hamlet around, undoing what he has ineptly done in the way of makeup and costume, answering his criticisms somewhat impatiently. At the other extreme from Olivier's players' reaction, the Player in W. S. Gilbert's *Rosencrantz and Guildenstern* tells Hamlet that the actors do not lecture *him* on "the duties of heirs-apparent," and that he also ought to confine himself to things he understands (Gilbert 86).

Every Hamlet is excited by the play's preparations, and the excitement is heightened by the play's paradoxical relation to the murder itself. On the one hand, the play distances the thought of Hamlet's father's murder because it represents the act only in a fiction, with other names, another locale, and various conventions intervening. But on the other hand, the play brings the murder closer and for Hamlet provides a way to assimilate the experience and make it more real. This closeness makes the Romantic Hamlet tremble with apprehension and sympathetic feeling. The Oedipal Hamlet is excited because he is going to symbolically kill his father, symbolically kill Claudius (because the revelation of his deed will be a kind of thrust at his life), and chasten his mother at the same time. In fact, the Oedipal Hamlet's preparations for the play have mostly concerned his mother, as we shall see. And the Hamlet of action and dispatch is excited because he is at last doing something, affecting events, and not least important, completely tipping his hand to Claudius. Along with these characters may be found the Hamlets whose excitement stems from fear or derangement.

The audience must be prepared also. Bringing a play into the play means rehearsing the spectators as well as the main performers. The most important members of the audience, Claudius and Gertrude, are "naturals" who need no coaching—can be given none in fact—but will be prompted by their past acts and their consciences. Hamlet now turns to the next most important spectator, Horatio.

Horatio is the least conspicuous of the major characters in *Hamlet,* though he appears in about half the scenes and has more lines than Gertrude, Ophelia, or Laertes (Spevack 828, 860, 866, 873). Horatio works best as part reflection and part complement to Hamlet's character. Sometimes the two act together—observing Claudius at the play, mocking Osric in 5.2. At other times one works as a check on the other, though unequally. Horatio unsuccessfully tries to restrain Hamlet from following the ghost in 1.4, from his display of passion at Ophelia's graveside in 5.1, from accepting Laertes' challenge in 5.2. Hamlet successfully restrains Horatio from suicide in 5.2. Horatio is the only one around whom Hamlet can trust. He is, as Hamlet points out at length here (acknowledging that he has gone on rather long at Horatio's praises by saying "Something too much of this" [71]), reliable because he is "not passion's slave" (69) in the play's world, where everyone else seems to Hamlet driven by ambition, lust, revenge, greed, or fear. Horatio will be a stronger character where Hamlet is weaker, and vice versa. But in one theatrical respect Horatio is constant: he is the character who represents us; as Bert O. States has put it, he serves as "a delegate or extension of the audience itself" (50). Horatio's skepticism about the ghost at the play's beginning was ours, and so was his transformation to belief as we saw the ghost's reality for ourselves, with him, "with the sensible and true avouch" (1.1.57) of his eyes and our own. We too, like Horatio, would like to put a rein on some of Hamlet's wilder rangings (as considering too curiously), and we too have been chastened by the reflection that there is more in heaven and earth than is dreamt of in our philosophy. We will be, with Horatio, somewhat appalled at Hamlet's sang-froid in sending Rosencrantz and Guildenstern to their deaths, though it will not bate our loyalty. And here, too, we feel he is speaking to us:

> There is a play to-night before the king.
> One scene of it comes near the circumstance
> Which I have told thee, of my father's death.
> I prithee, when thou seest that act afoot,
> Even with the very comment of thy soul
> Observe my uncle. If his occulted guilt
> Do not itself unkennel in one speech,
> It is a damnèd ghost that we have seen,
> And my imaginations are as foul
> As Vulcan's stithy. Give him heedful note,
> For I mine eyes will rivet to his face,
> And after we will both our judgments join
> In censure of his seeming.
>
> (72–84)

When Horatio agrees, Hamlet has completed preparations for the performers and the audience. The king and queen enter, and Hamlet tells Horatio he must be "idle" (usually glossed as *foolish, mad*). Hamlet does change his behavior in turning from the players and Horatio, with whom he has been direct and unquibbling, to the court party.

The Play within the Play

Hamlet's strategy with everyone except the players and Horatio is to take the sense of what they say and twist it; to equivocate on the sense of a word like *fares,* as in his first exchange with Claudius:

KING. How fares our cousin Hamlet?
HAMLET. Excellent, i'faith, of the chameleon's dish. I eat
    the air, promise-crammed. You cannot feed capons so.
KING. I have nothing with this answer, Hamlet. These
    words are not mine.
HAMLET. No, nor mine now.

(89–94)

It has been his way earlier, with Polonius. It is the way of fools
and clowns, in fact of the First Clown in 5.1. But there is more
equivocation here than meets the eye: Hamlet's ambition is not
the only referent for his being "promise-crammed," and "You
are the most immediate to our throne" (1.2.109) is not the only
promise of the play. Hamlet has also promised to remember
the ghost, to avenge his father, and as yet that promise lacks
fulfillment. But Claudius understands by these words Hamlet's
lack of advancement only (and see Hamlet's words at 326).

The exchange with Polonius, leading up to the worst pun
in the play ("It was a brute part of him to kill so capital a calf
there"—101), is time-filling for both the apprehensive and the
action-loving Hamlets, who leave Polonius with relief at the
favorable answer to "Be the players ready?" But the Oedipal
Hamlet is more purposeful in his continued mocking of Polonius, whom he will not let go from his fooling until the old
man is dead. Polonius is seen by this Hamlet as the author of
his daughter's weaknesses, and since Ophelia shares these
with all women and with Gertrude in particular, Polonius is
obscurely to blame for Gertrude's failings and stands for all
fathers.

Hamlet turns his attention next to Ophelia. It must be admitted that the dialogue between Hamlet and Ophelia at the
play is troublesome for those with a univalent interpretation of
Hamlet. Ophelia is at once too innocent and too knowing, too
aloof and too playful, while Hamlet is both too cruel to Ophelia
and too amusing in a way that Ophelia recognizes. Here is the
first exchange:

HAMLET. Lady, shall I lie in your lap?
OPHELIA. No, my lord.

HAMLET. I mean, my head upon your lap?
OPHELIA. Ay, my lord.
HAMLET. Do you think I meant country matters?
OPHELIA. I think nothing, my lord.
HAMLET. That's a fair thought to lie between maids' legs.
OPHELIA. What is, my lord?
HAMLET. Nothing.
OPHELIA. You are merry, my lord.
HAMLET. Who, I?
OPHELIA. Ay, my lord.
HAMLET. O God, your only jig-maker! What should a man
    do but be merry? For look you how cheerfully my
    mother looks, and my father died within's two hours.
OPHELIA. Nay, 'tis twice two months, my lord.
HAMLET. So long? Nay then, let the devil wear black.

                                            (107–23)

Ophelia's innocence, scandalized by the suggestion that Hamlet
lie *in her lap*, is yet a little too quick to think his meaning the
bawdy rather than the accepted, innocent sense of lying at her
feet with his head in her lap; Steevens demonstrated long ago
the commonness of the practice, and of Hamlet's expression for
it, at private shows of this sort (Furness 238). Looked at in this
way, Ophelia is the one who turns the conversation to country
matters. Hamlet says, "Be not you ashamed to show, he'll not
shame to tell you what it means" (136–38) and Ophelia knows
he is being "naught." Later she appreciates his wit as "keen,"
and even joins the punning in giving her critical opinion: when
he says to her *keen*, "It would cost you a groaning to take off my
edge," she calls it "Still better, and worse" (239–41). This par-
ticipation of Ophelia in the bawdy wordplay is embarrassing for
those who want her to be the complete innocent. Thus Olivier,
as he reduces the play to dumb show only, cuts and rearranges
the dialogue:

        HAMLET. Is this a prologue, or the posy of a ring?
        OPHELIA. 'Tis brief, my lord.
        HAMLET. As woman's love.
        OPHELIA. [tearfully] You are keen, my lord, you are keen.
        HAMLET. It would cost you a groaning to take off my edge.
                                            (143–45, 239–40)

Jean Simmons, Olivier's very blonde and very innocent Ophelia, does not reply as the dumb show begins. Even Rodney Bennett, in the almost complete BBC Shakespeare Plays *Hamlet,* cuts the lines at 239–41 about the keenness and groaning, perhaps for economy, but perhaps to spare Lalla Ward, his frail and weak Ophelia, having to say such sharp things.

But the hard-case Ophelia described by Madariaga or portrayed by Marianne Faithfull in Richardson's *Hamlet* must downplay or ignore some of the text also. Though Hamlet suggests all sorts of knowingness about Ophelia, yet everything he says indicates that he thinks her virginal: "That's a fair thought to lie between maids' legs. . . . It would cost you a groaning to take off my edge." Moreover, that she is intelligent enough to pick up on some of his language hardly makes her a slut. Her respectfulness is constrained, after all, because she speaks to a prince, whom she milords at every line in their first exchange, though mercifully not throughout the rest of the scene. She may even, like Lalla Ward's Ophelia, smile at Hamlet's witticisms while thinking them more frightening than funny, and respond solely out of obligation.

Ophelia has a part which may be played as an absolute innocent, and if it is played thus, we will be the more intrigued by the fact that her every appearance is the cue for talk about sex. When we first see her the talk is all of precautions to keep her virginity; at her next appearance Hamlet questions her chastity and talks about women's affectations and paintings. When we next see her, at the play, he comments on the pain it would cost her to give up her virginity, among other "country matters." At her final appearance she sings of deflowered maids and young men who "will do't if they come to't" (4.5.60).

As to Hamlet and his motives, he may not need justification for them. He may merely be having a pleasant time with Ophelia; Eric Partridge points out how frequently in Shakespeare and other Elizabethan authors we find "men and women conversing together on intimate subjects and making the most erotic innuendoes and the most doubtful puns" (38). If Hamlet is hurting Ophelia deliberately, he may be doing so for various reasons that we looked at in 3.1. He may also be oblivious to whether he is hurting her or not, because he is concentrating on his mother, because he is concentrating on the king, or because he is mad: "For look you how cheerfully my mother looks, and my father died within's two hours" (120–21). When Ophelia corrects Hamlet by telling him it has been "twice two months" since the death of his father, Hamlet shortens the time again in his reply: "O heavens! die two months ago, and not forgotten yet?" (124–25). However Hamlet is played in this scene it must be with excitement and impatience until the play has its desired effect.

The dumb show begins at 129. There is one perennial question about this scene: why does Claudius not react to the poisoning in the dumb show instead of waiting until 120 lines later, when Lucianus speaks and Hamlet interrupts the action to summarize the rest of the play? The dumb show directions seem clear enough. Either the show is not so immediately comprehensible to Claudius as it seems to us, or Claudius is not paying attention (Dover Wilson's answer), or he *does* understand but does not react visibly. However stylized the dumb show may be made, it still seems as if it ought to be comprehensible to a man for whom the act of poisoning is so significant. But if it is not only stylized but comic, then its sting may be removed so that Claudius laughs before taking any offense. One stage tradition has the dumb show played in great comic exaggeration by clowns, and the dialogue spoken with inflated expression and gesture; in other words, the players proceed to do everything that Hamlet has told them not to do. When the little play veers from naturalism, its parody may point in either direction—toward the art of the theater or toward the life of the castle or of the mind. Thus Jack Jorgens describes the *commedia* style play within the play in Richardson's *Hamlet:* "a parodic event in which Claudius becomes a red-nosed clown, Elsinore a flimsy cardboard castle, the cuckolding of King Hamlet a game of sexual leapfrog between the Queen of Hearts and her two royal studs, and the murder a festive dance around the Maypole turned grotesque as the King is strangled in the brightly colored streamers and the self-crowned murderer leaps into the Queen's arms—its strength and truth is its duplicating in terms of visual style the insane discord in Hamlet's mind" (34–35). Richardson, like Olivier, does not separate the dumb show from the play. In both film versions Claudius is forced to take notice. But the dumb show need not be so obtrusive as in these interpretations. If the king and queen are joking or petting, either may miss the poisoning, especially if the dumb show is played rapidly. Hamlet's reaction to the brief prologue, "Is this a prologue, or the posy of a ring?" can be impatience at the players, because Hamlet had hoped to have the poisoning reiterated three times, in show, prologue, and play, and his shaft has already missed twice; or it may merely be Hamlet's enjoying himself now the thing is underway and he is assured that Claudius, though he may not have reacted to the dumb show, will yet be hit before the play is over.

Even if Claudius has seen and understood the poisoning in the dumb show, he may well be concealing his knowledge so that he may test Hamlet to see whether this has been a setup: "Have you heard the argument? . . . What do you call the play?" (224, 228). And finally, Claudius's lack of reaction to the dumb show and his later violent reaction may be a confirmation of Hamlet's wisdom in pleading for naturalism from the players: Claudius may recognize, but is not touched by the stylized representation of the poisoning in the dumb show, but when he sees and hears the act in more realistic guise, he is "tented to the quick," as Hamlet has planned at 2.2.583.

At the very heart of *Hamlet*, the Player King begins to speak, describing a situation that is partly like that of Gertrude and old Hamlet (thirty years of marriage, the wonted garden nap) and partly unlike it (his infirmity, the murderer who is a nephew rather than a brother). A convention of rhyme distinguishes the speech of the inner play from that of the larger one. Hamlet has twice said that his object in presenting the play is to unkennel Claudius's guilt, but most of what is said in the little play seems more likely to affect Gertrude.

When her husband says she will remarry after his death, the Player Queen interrupts to say remarrying would be like killing her first husband. "That's wormwood" (173), says Hamlet. He may be speaking of the Queen's protest itself, hopefully but futilely, since the strong and sensual Gertrude is untouched by these lines, her nature assuring her that there is nothing ill in remarrying. Hamlet may be commenting on Gertrude's reaction (or Claudius's reaction): some Gertrudes will wince at the Player Queen's lines and the Gertrude who is accessory to old Hamlet's death may wince doubly here.

The Player King replies with a worldly speech that echoes many of Hamlet's remarks in the play, though it contradicts Hamlet's feelings about the remarriage of his mother (I do not intend to enter the debate about whether this or some other passage is Hamlet's inserted "speech of some dozen or sixteen lines"—2.2.526). Memory and passion end; grief and joy, like the world itself, pass. "This world is not for aye" (192)—("Ay, madam, it is common" [1.2.74]; "get you to my lady's chamber, and tell her, let her paint an inch thick, to this favor she must come" [5.1.180–83]). So pass love and fortune. "The great man down, you mark his favorite flies, / The poor advanced makes friends of enemies" (196–97)—("those that would make mows at him while my father lived give . . . . a hundred ducats for his picture in little" [2.2.356–58]).

The Player Queen answers that she should be deprived of food, light, freedom, and rest if she ever remarries. Hamlet's "If she should break it now!" at 216 *may* be ironic: he knows the outcome in this play and in the play he acts in—that is, "real life," where Gertrude has not mourned as long as "a beast that wants discourse of reason" (1.2.150) would have. So Gielgud played the line in his 1936 production, as if equivalent to "What absurd sentimentalities! . . . What old-fashioned non-sense!" (Gilder 76). But Hamlet may be in earnest. The little play is the past, which Gertrude and Claudius may resist entering, but Hamlet wishes to enter and to change or arrest.

As the Player King sleeps and the Player Queen exits, Hamlet turns from her to the real queen. Hamlet might reason-

ably be more concerned with how Claudius likes the play than
with how Gertrude does. One Hamlet *is* more concerned with
Claudius, but speaks to his mother, consciously avoiding his
real object and hoping to provoke him, as indeed he does:
Claudius starts to question Hamlet. Another Hamlet, the
Oedipal one, speaks to his mother because she is his real concern. "Madam, how like you this play?" he asks (221), knowing how she likes it because he has not taken his eyes from her
face during the dialogue. For whatever this Hamlet has said in
soliloquy and to Horatio, he has planned the play from the
beginning to affect Gertrude rather than Claudius. "The lady
doth protest too much, methinks" (222). The sensual and self-
knowing Gertrude responds thus cynically: only a naif would
suppose a woman in such circumstances would not remarry.
The pleasure-loving, but weak, Gertrude who lacks self-knowl-
edge answers in the spirit of the dramatic spectacle—she
knows from watching the dumb show that the Player Queen
will accept the second lover, and true to her nature, she makes
no application of the Player Queen's situation to herself. She
does not take personally representations of sin and weakness;
she is not moved to think of the state of her soul by any casual
reference to death. Neither of these Gertrudes has too many
thorns lodged in her bosom to prick and sting her (1.5.87–88);
neither's conscience is easily aroused. A third Gertrude *has*
been affected by the play, and responds nervously. She cannot
say the Player Queen ought to agree with her husband; she
cannot second the woman's oath either, since her own situation glaringly shows that love changes with fortune.

Hamlet's "O, but she'll keep her word" (223) stressed on
she'll and/or *her*, says indirectly to Gertrude what Hamlet has
not yet been able to say about her faithlessness to old Hamlet.
He is rehearsing now for the scene in which he will chide her
directly for that faithlessness. But stressed on *keep* the line
points in a different direction: Hamlet is saying, "Don't be so
cynical; women may be faithful," or even, "This time she *will*
be faithful."

Claudius's questions to Hamlet (224–25, 228) seem disingenuous if the king has seen the prologue. If he has not, he may not know or suspect what is coming. If he has seen it, we must suppose a Claudius who with cool control probes Hamlet to make sure the play's resemblance to the Elsinore murder is not accidental. This Claudius, as Roy Walker points out, is not frightened by Hamlet's knowledge of his murder nor by Hamlet himself, and when he rushes from the play it is solely his own act that has frightened him (74).

Lucianus enters at 235 and Hamlet not only introduces him but prompts his speech at 244. Hamlet's solecism about ravens bellowing for revenge does not make immediate sense in the context—a commentator a century ago noted that the line is a conflation of two lines from a play on Richard the Third (Furness 257). But the speech works as private code for Hamlet, Claudius, and the audience, reminding us that the play within the play can be a projection as well as a history. The little play looks backward to a murder of a brother, but in the relationship of Lucianus to the King and in Hamlet's seemingly inappropriate remark, it also looks forward to the revenge of a nephew on an uncle.

Lucianus speaks his lines and pours the poison into the Player King's ears. Hamlet cannot resist jumping in again:

> 'A poisons him i' th' garden for his estate. His name's Gonzago. The story is extant, and written in very choice Italian. You shall see anon how the murtherer gets the love of Gonzago's wife. (251–54)

Hamlet has his triple iteration of the poisoning and the widow-murderer match after all: in dumb show, action with dialogue, and his own commentary. In one way of playing these lines, Claudius, intent in conversation with Gertrude or caresses, has missed *both* the dumb show poisoning and the words and actions of Lucianus. Finally Hamlet grabs his head, turns it toward the tableau of Lucianus and the dying King, and shouts the lines at 251–54.

Claudius reacts. He need do no more than rise to justify anything Horatio and Hamlet say of his response afterward

(277–80), but the effect on his conscience (we will not see the whole effect until the next scene) can warrant more violent reactions. We may see the range of possibilities in the symmetrically opposed renderings of the scene in the Olivier and BBC versions. In Olivier's film, Basil Sydney grows increasingly agitated during the little play (all in dumb show) until he finally rises, shielding his eyes from the players with his fists, and shouts in anguish "Give me some light!" Olivier triumphantly carries a torch across the room and thrusts it toward the king's face, laughing as he does so. According to Sir John Gielgud, Sarah Bernhardt is supposed to have invented this bit of business (Gilder 150). Tyrone Guthrie had George Grizzard use a spotlight in a similar way in his modern-dress 1963 Minneapolis production (Rossi 80). In the Olivier version, Claudius, taking his hands away from his face, looks at the torch, looks at Hamlet, then thrusts the torch from him, shouting "Away!" He turns, gathers his robes, and runs from the room. In the BBC television play, Patrick Stewart stands up at the conclusion of line 254, but in anger rather than anguish. He asks coolly for light, extending his arm toward a servant with a torch, but not taking his eyes from Derek Jacobi. He then thrusts the torch at Hamlet's face. Hamlet covers his face in fear, then, when nothing further happens, peeks from between his hands, giggles nervously, and finally laughs maniacally as Claudius turns, commands "Away!" and leaves.

Hamlet and the Recorders

Again Hamlet speaks to us in speaking to Horatio: "Didst perceive. . . . Upon the talk of the poisoning?" (277,279). Hamlet exults in his triumph, sings, calls for music. These lines before Rosencrantz and Guildenstern enter can convey unalloyed exultation, the nervous merrymaking of the adolescent who knows he is misbehaving, or knowledge of triumph tinged with fear at what he has had to reveal in order to triumph. With Rosencrantz and Guildenstern, Hamlet continues his equivocation on words like *choler, wildly,* and *wholesome,* as he had done while assuming his "antic disposition." But he also mocks Guildenstern's style of speech, both by imitation ("Your wisdom should show itself more richer to signify this to the doctor" [292–93]) and more directly ("I do not well understand that" [336]); he calls the relation between himself and the two men "trade" (320), and he tells them he cannot understand their inability to play the recorder ("It is as easy as lying" [343]) and warns them away from their attempts to sound him. All of this usually plays rather grimly: after all, Hamlet is telling them they are not very clever, commercial, lying spies in enough ways that they can hardly fail to understand. He has already dangerously tipped his hand to Claudius and may assume Rosencrantz and Guildenstern will report these words as well. But the other side of the encounter is the glee with which Hamlet has seen his Mousetrap sprung and the verbal fireworks with which he mocks Guildenstern and Rosencrantz's unwillingness to say in any straightforward way that the king and queen are angry.

Polonius enters to repeat the summons from the queen, and Hamlet tests how far Polonius will go in humoring him. This may be the scene Johnson had in mind when he said that "the pretended madness of Hamlet causes much mirth" (196). If so, he must have been describing the reaction of others, not himself, to a rather unfunny exchange. The "wittiness" of Hamlet's jests is proportioned to the wit of the targets. Hamlet dismisses everyone at 372.

Hamlet's soliloquy indicates his resolve to act now that he knows the king's guilt—"Now could I drink hot blood / And do such bitter business as the day / Would quake to look on" (375–77)—but it can also be read as bravado or even as the culmination of an excitement that must disperse: only by being so worked up could Hamlet act, and only for the moment it lasts. Two points in the soliloquy deserve attention. One is the reference to gaping tombs and contagion from hell that opens it. Hamlet worried at the end of 2.2 that the ghost might be a spirit come from hell to trick him into damnation. Now he speaks in despite of hell's contagion, or perhaps with the idea that the night's evil somehow helps his purpose. This aspect of Hamlet, deriving from the conventions of revenge tragedy, will be moderated or highlighted in production as the particular reading of Hamlet's character dictates. *Hamlet* is so subtle a revenge tragedy that its hero can do all his bloody work and still be clean at the play's end. But Hamlet can also be played as a revenger more strongly in the tradition, who starts to feel here the thirst for blood and who, before the play's end, if he has not become a villain, has at least been sullied with the deceit and corruption he set out to fight. Hamlet's linking of hell's contagion with his own purposes fits with other references to himself as prompted by both heaven and hell to his revenge (2.2.570), and points forward to his reason for not killing Claudius at 3.3.74.

The other point that we may observe about the soliloquy is that although it begins with revenge, which we might presume to be foremost in Hamlet's mind after the successful springing of the Mousetrap, yet most of it concerns his mother. Fredson Bowers argues that the whole of Hamlet's speech about his mother here is necessary to warn the audience, to prevent its believing, as Gertrude does, that Hamlet means to do her harm in the closet scene (215–17). The Oedipal Hamlet of course will not only emphasize those lines which deal with Gertrude but will also link them suggestively with the violence Hamlet is now ready to inflict on his father surrogate. Nor will he ignore the connection between his intentions toward them and the contagion of hell with which he began his speech.

Scene Three

We can here see for ourselves the "distemper" of the king reported by Guildenstern a hundred lines back. Claudius tells us for the second time (cf. 3.1.168ff.) of his plan to send Hamlet to England. There is no talk now of Hamlet's danger to himself or to anyone other than the king. Claudius defends his decision by his position: because he is king he may not endure the danger Hamlet offers. We may easily imagine that Rosencrantz and Guildenstern have just reported Hamlet's words about lacking advancement. They are told to prepare themselves:

> I your commission will forthwith dispatch,
> And he to England shall along with you.
>
> (3–4)

If line 3 is to tell us Rosencrantz and Guildenstern know that their commission includes a request for the English king to kill Hamlet (Moberly first made the suggestion—Furness 274), they must make some extraordinary acknowledgment, like (at least momentary) horror. They then recover and give the two speeches from 7 to 23. Their speeches are in any case rationalizations of the king's line about "the terms of our estate"; that is, they attempt to justify Claudius's fear of Hamlet and the king's assigning his own actions to some motive that looks like national security. Guildenstern says that the king's "hazard" poses a general danger:

> Most holy and religious fear it is
> To keep those many many bodies safe
> That live and feed upon your majesty.
>
> (8–10)

Rosencrantz's metaphors comparing majesty to a "gulf" or whirlpool and a massy wheel (15–22) amplify what his companion has said about the dependence of the subjects on the king's safety. If they know or guess what is planned for Hamlet the speeches are also attempts to justify their own actions, since their knowledge makes them accessories. A more traditional reading makes them ignorant of the commission's lethal intent; Claudius may in fact not yet have determined to have Hamlet killed. Their speeches can be read as political commonplaces pronounced hesitatingly—even almost distastefully—or as just toadying, but not necessarily with any knowledge that Hamlet will be more than temporarily banished.

Aside from the fact that the sentiments are commonplaces, we should also remember how Hamlet's recent actions might strike those without intimate knowledge of the ghost and his message. Hamlet has offered for public view a play in which one man kills another for his crown and wife; or, to look at it differently, a play in which a nephew kills an uncle for his crown. Hamlet has, from the view of one unacquainted with any evidence of old Hamlet's murder, accused, insulted, or threatened Claudius. Rosencrantz and Guildenstern he has merely insulted.

Whatever reassurance or confirmation the speeches of Hamlet's old school friends are intended to offer Claudius, they cannot help reminding us, and Claudius as well, that the reliance of the "many many bodies" on the king's welfare makes the murder of a king that much more heinous:

> Never alone
> Did the king sigh, but with a general groan.
> (22–23)

Claudius dismisses Rosencrantz and Guildenstern with images of warfare and imprisonment:

> Arm you, I pray you, to this speedy voyage,
> For we will fetters put upon this fear,
> Which now goes too free-footed.
> (24–26)

Polonius enters at 27 to remind us of his plan to eavesdrop at Hamlet's meeting with his mother. At once it is unclear whether Hamlet or Gertrude is the object of his spying:

> I'll warrant she'll tax him home,
> And as you said, and wisely was it said,
> 'Tis meet that some more audience than a mother,
> Since nature makes them partial, should o'erhear
> The speech
> (29–33)

That the interview is no longer useful to Claudius, that Hamlet will work his intent on his mother rather than vice versa, and that Polonius's last spying scene will kill him—these are all ironies that one who knows the play will feel here, but the main feeling is one of impatience for Polonius to leave and for the king, alone, to reveal himself in soliloquy.

At this point, once Polonius is offstage, Patrick Stewart, in the BBC teleplay, suddenly sobs: he has suppressed every reaction but anger at the little play in the previous scene, and now some release is necessary. Claudius, whatever turn we give his character, has been a social man, a man of action rather than reflection. We remember speeches where he boldly repeats the circumstances of his coming to the throne before the assembled nobles; where he explains to Hamlet, in his smoothest paternal-avuncular style, how dead fathers must be forgotten; where he dispatches or receives ambassadors; and, later, where he turns Laertes' threat into his own weapon against Hamlet. When he turns from his usual traffic with others to reflection, it is not surprising that his mode of thought should be dialectical. Like Hotspur, another active man who, when stymied, thinks he could divide himself and "go to buffets" (1 Henry IV 2.3.29), Claudius has a psychomachic confrontation with himself, or, if not precisely a battle between two parts of his soul, at least a conversation with question and answer.

His offense is a brother's murder, and he wishes to pray and be forgiven:

> Pray can I not,
> Though inclination be as sharp as will.
> My stronger guilt defeats my strong intent,
> And like a man to double business bound
> I stand in pause where I shall first begin,
> And both neglect.
>
> (38–43)

The battle is metaphorically present in guilt's "defeat" of intent. The speech goes on, not as if Claudius were a man with two tasks, but as if he were two men. The first asks whether there is rain enough in the heavens to cleanse the blood from his hands, and then moves from this figurative question to literal ones: what is the purpose of mercy except to be used on the sinful? for what do we pray but to be spared temptation and delivered from evil, having fallen? This first voice is hopeful. But a despairing voice answers that the penitent cannot ask forgiveness while holding on to the gains of sin, and asks a question in turn: "May one be pardoned and retain th' offense?" The hopeful voice makes a rather cynical observation here:

> In the corrupted currents of this world
> Offense's gilded hand may shove by justice,
> And oft 'tis seen the wicked prize itself
> Buys out the law.
>
> (57–60)

If this is intended as consolation for a more permanent loss, it fails: the despairing voice answers that there is no such trickery at judgment, where the accused must stand witness against himself. This voice goes on to ask what then remains, and the hopeful voice answers, "Try what repentance can. What can it not?" But the despairing voice comes back to the strain with which it began: "Yet what can it when one cannot repent?"

> *Despair*
>
> O wretched state! O bosom black as death!
> O limèd soul, that struggling to be free
> Art more engaged!
>
> *Hope*
>   Help, angels! Make assay.
> Bow, stubborn knees, and, heart with strings of steel,
> Be soft as sinews of the new-born babe.
> All may be well.
>
> (67–72)

Hope has the last word, and till the end of the scene, we, like Hamlet, can be fooled into supposing that Claudius is successfully praying (if such a phrase may be pardoned).

A confirmation of the way Claudius's speech must have been delivered in Shakespeare's theater, as a dialogue between Hope and Despair, is offered by the memorial reconstruction of it that exists in the first Quarto of the play. There, in part, Claudius's speech reads as follows:

O these are sinnes that are vnpardonable:
Why say thy sinnes are blacker than is ieat,
Yet may contrition make them as white as snowe:
I but still to perseuer in a sinne,
It is an act gainst the vniuersall power,
Most wretched man, stoope, bend thee to thy prayer,
Aske grace of heauen to keepe thee from despaire.

(1417–23)

Even though the actors who put together the corrupt text of the
first Quarto have reduced the language of Claudius's speech to
the conventions of black as jet and white as snow (the latter,
after all, does appear in the authentic texts), they have preserved the form of the speech.

The style of this speech is also a reflection of its matter. Its
straightforwardness contrasts with Claudius's earlier rhetori-
cally weighted pronouncements, as in the oxymorons of his
first speech. As at judgment, so in this speech, "There is no
shuffling." This combination of sincerity and anguish brings us
into momentary sympathy with Claudius.

What is the relevance of these formal and stylistic glances
for our main topic? Whatever the form of the speech, how do
different Claudiuses read it? However many ways the king's
part may be read, this speech divides the interpretations into
only two groups. These may be seen as weak or strong, more
or less fearful, more or less sympathetic, or opposed in other
ways, but the distinguishing feature is the moral depth given
the character. For one Claudius, the speech is prompted by ter-
ror of hell and the conviction that he will be damned. Beyond
the incidents of the little play, he has seen in it a message to his
guilty soul that murder will out, blood will have blood, retribution waits. Hamlet's knowledge of his crime and even public
discovery are not of much matter to him at this moment. But
his offense "smells to heaven" and will call down punishment
worse than that of Cain. For the other Claudius, Hamlet's
knowledge and the possibility of public exposure are even less
important at this moment. This Claudius also fears punishment, but he has a conscience which goes beyond fear of

punishment and hope of reward. For him, the speech expresses remorse arising out of a real moral sense. The play
showed him what a heinous act the killing of a man is, as he
had not seen it before, from the outside. Rosencrantz and
Guildenstern unwittingly stung him further by reminding him
that everyone's welfare depends on the king's, and he recalls it
was a king he killed. He begins his soliloquy by acknowledging
that the murder was that of a brother. We are reminded of the
ghost's characterization of the deed:

> Murther most foul, as in the best it is,
> But this most foul, strange, and unnatural.
>
> (1.5.27–28)

If we have sympathy with Macbeth struggling with the temptation to kill his kinsman, king, and guest, our feelings about
Claudius here are somewhat more complicated. Claudius has
already acted. We can feel at best a kind of retrospective sympathy. But the speech of this Claudius taps the guilt, remorse,
and consciousness of continued sin in all of us—with that we
must sympathize.

Robert G. Hunter, in *Shakespeare and the Mystery of God's
Judgments*, anticipates my method with an interesting variation: he introduces another character into the play—God—
who although he has no lines still has a range of possible interpretations. It is God whose plan calls for Claudius's ultimate
punishment, and God who uses Hamlet as sometimes unwilling agent. The reasons for Claudius's failure to repent depend
on our interpretation of what sort of God we have in our production. Hunter gives two readings:

> If the God of the play is Augustine's God, he has
> foreseen that Claudius will be unable to yield his consent to
> God's summons, but the failure is of Claudius's will, and
> God's justice working through Hamlet presents Claudius
> with this opportunity to exercise his free will. However, this
> mysterious but comparatively benevolent deity is not
> insisted on by the play. It is simultaneously and equally
> possible to interpret Claudius's failure to repent as evidence

that the God of the play is Calvin's God, who has willed the
reprobation of Claudius, willed his attempt to repent and its
failure, withheld from eternity the grace that Claudius
vainly seeks. (111)

Hamlet's speech is also a dialogue or debate of sorts: "and
am I then revenged . . . ? / No" (84,87). Hamlet stands at a fork
in the road. Either path he chooses will lead to important consequences. It is a wonderful emblematic moment for art and
for drama: Hamlet, sword out, bloodthirsty, and with a desire
for revenge so profound he wishes not only to destroy
Claudius but to send him to hell, stands behind Claudius, who
is shorn for the moment of all his self-command, his deceit,
and perhaps his self-deceit, and who is trying desperately to
repent and pray. It is an emblem for drama because it has the
elements of performance within performance. Claudius tries to
pray; Hamlet is audience to this and therefore seemingly more
aware, in the way dramatic audiences are supposed to be more
aware than those they observe, of what is going on. We look on
at both scenes and are seemingly best informed of all. But all of
this blows up as soon as Hamlet, having made his decision,
leaves, and we discover that the least aware was in fact the
most aware, that Claudius has been unable to pray, and that
we and Hamlet have been deceived. The moment both re-
verses and fulfills dramatic irony. It becomes a special emblem
for *Hamlet*, rather than drama in general, an emblem of mis-
conception, failed intention, mystery, and surprise.

It is not difficult to read this speech as showing Hamlet
simply unable to kill Claudius. He has an opportunity: he recognizes it, determines to do it, and then *in the middle of the
second line* he is already thinking of the consequences in such a
way as to prevent his acting. The impediment may be the
Oedipal problem that by killing Claudius, Hamlet would be
attacking himself (since their love for Gertrude and their desire
to get a rival for her affection out of the way unite Hamlet and
Claudius), or cowardice, a soul unfit for such action, or some
other disabling motive. But Hamlet can also be seen here as the
revenger in the tradition, thirsting for blood, but eager for an

ultimate revenge: to see his adversary in hell. Hamlet has already spoken of his purposes as linked not only with heaven's, but also with hell's, at 2.2.570 and 3.2.375. This is the Hamlet that made Johnson cringe, and the speech he found "too horrible to be read or to be uttered" (193).

Some interpreters have felt the need for an external reason for Hamlet's sudden pause in the middle of his second line. Thus Olivier suddenly sees the icon of a saint on the altar where Claudius kneels in prayer. Kozintsev has his Hamlet raise his sword and see the cross of the hilt before he speaks the line "And so 'a goes to heaven" (74). Jacobi simply pauses in thought.

Every Hamlet is misled by what he sees, thinking that Claudius will go to heaven if he is killed while praying. The irony of Hamlet's mistake is made explicit in his words about his father's state of soul: "And how his audit stands, who knows save heaven?" (82). But whether he is "encroaching on the role of providence" and playing at God by presuming to decide the issue of Claudius's salvation, as Maynard Mack suggests in "The World of Hamlet" (521), or whether he is merely offering excuses for an inability or unwillingness to act, Hamlet spares Claudius. He exits, and Claudius rises to tell us of his unsuccessful prayer.

Scene Four

Scene Four continues the sequence of "showings" and playlets we have seen in the previous three scenes. Here one main arranged overhearing turns into three shows. In the first, Polonius is the sole onstage spectator or listener for the beginning of Hamlet's interview with his mother. Following Gertrude's alarm, Polonius mistakes the intent of Hamlet. We have been warned by Hamlet that the meeting may include a certain amount of frightening but harmless acting on his part—speaking daggers, but using none (at least toward his mother). Polonius has not been so warned, and finds that his role as audience may involve some danger.

Hamlet goes on to present the second show to Gertrude: he says he is setting up a mirror where she may see the inmost part of her; she says he turns her eyes into her very soul. This show displays Gertrude's conscience, as the last scene displayed Claudius's, but hers is not a self-examination, as is usually the case with soul-searching. Hamlet is shining the lights into corners and setting up the mirror, holding Gertrude's face to the view.

The third show is also solely for one onstage spectator. The ghost appears to whet Hamlet's "almost blunted purpose." We have seen cases where spectators were informed, misinformed (Hamlet in 3.3), or uninformed by the shows they observed (some of the watchers of the play within the play). Some of the spectators were legitimate audiences, others were spies, still others, accidental witnesses of a scene (Marcellus and Bernardo) or corroborative ones (Horatio in 1.1 and 3.2). Gertrude, at the ghost's appearance here, is the first instance of a character who *cannot* be a spectator at an important show. Her inability to see the ghost is one of the defining features of her character.

In the Folio, Gertrude does not exit when Hamlet drags Polonius away, so that the scene includes what is conventionally numbered as 4.1. Thus a fourth show succeeds the others: Gertrude's description of what has taken place and Claudius's reaction to Polonius's death. But I have followed the Quarto and most modern editors in treating this as a cleared stage and a scene break.

"Thou find'st to be too busy is some danger"

At the beginning of this scene Polonius instructs Gertrude about her behavior to her son. Then Hamlet speaks before his entrance (only in the Folio): "Mother, mother, mother!" (6). Olivier takes advantage of the ability of film to crosscut, showing two places at once: he speaks the line in a hesitant and childish fashion while climbing the huge stairs to his mother's bedroom, thus setting up the Oedipal confrontation in which he will range between infant son and dominating lover. Burton, who *is* offstage in a filmed stageplay that uses no crosscutting or other filmic devices, repeats "mother" loudly, staccato—one of those continued repetitions of a word that eventually results in the word's seeming to lose all meaning; there is an echo in these three *mothers* of "We shall obey, were she ten times our mother" (3.2.319). Polonius hides and a stichomythic exchange takes place:

> QUEEN.   Hamlet, thou hast thy father much offended.
> HAMLET.   Mother, you have my father much offended.
> QUEEN.   Come, come, you answer with an idle tongue.
> HAMLET.   Go, go, you question with a wicked [Folio *an idle*]
>   tongue.
>
> (10–13)

Hamlet's response in the formal second person to his mother's use of the familiar may be played as distancing, though in fact he is punctilious in never using the familiar with her. Usually her second line comes back very quickly and sharply (thus Claire Bloom in the BBC *Hamlet* and Eileen Herlie in both the Olivier and the Burton versions), but she may as easily be stopped momentarily by Hamlet's shift in the reference of *father* to her former husband.

> QUEEN.   Why, how now, Hamlet?
> HAMLET.   What's the matter now?
> QUEEN.   Have you forgot me?
> HAMLET.   No, by the rood, not so!
>   You are the queen, your husband's brother's wife,
>   And (would it were not so) you are my mother.
>
> (14–17)

She seems surprised at his accusation of wickedness, as she seems surprised later when he talks of killing a king. He reminds her of the multiple relationship (and thus of the technical incest): "your husband's brother's wife." At this point Jacobi's Hamlet gets a slap from Claire Bloom's Gertrude.

The interview so far, from the perspective of Gertrude or the listening Polonius, has demonstrated the perceptiveness of her earlier view of Hamlet's state of mind: "I doubt it is no other but the main, / His father's death and our o'erhasty marriage" (2.2.56–57). But the heat of Hamlet's feeling, the stirrings of her own conscience, her awareness of the listening Polonius, or some other cause makes her unwilling to continue the interview, and she attempts to leave. Hamlet restrains her, she cries out in fear, Polonius echoes her cry for help, and Hamlet stabs him through the arras, all in a few seconds.

Is Hamlet convinced the listener is Claudius when he thrusts through the arras?

> QUEEN.   O me, what hast thou done?
> HAMLET. Nay, I know not. Is it the king?
> QUEEN.   O, what a rash and bloody deed is this!
> HAMLET. A bloody deed—almost as bad, good mother,
>   As kill a king, and marry with his brother.
>
> (26–30)

That he has killed the king is his first thought. When Gertrude calls it a rash and bloody deed, he retorts that this regicide is almost as bad as regicide and incest together. But a less sane Hamlet will not answer in the same way; for him the possibility that the listener is Claudius is merely wild and wishful. He answers that it is a bloody deed: this killing (whoever it is) is almost as bad as killing a king and marrying his brother, another wild shot for which Hamlet has no grounds and a suspicion for which he never gives another indication.

Hamlet's victim is not Claudius but Polonius, whose death he acknowledges without a word of remorse:

> Thou wretched, rash, intruding fool, farewell!
> I took thee for thy better. Take thy fortune.
> Thou find'st to be too busy is some danger.
>
> (32–34)

Most commentators are more intent on explaining how we, the audience, are to take these lines than how Hamlet is to speak them. Thus Robert Ornstein, in *The Moral Vision of Jacobean*

Tragedy, tells us that Hamlet's behavior here is one of the tests of our sympathy with his character:

> Through his consummate artistry Shakespeare creates within us a sympathy with Hamlet which becomes almost an act of faith—a confidence in the untouched and untouchable core of his spiritual nature. This act of faith, renewed by the great speeches throughout the play, allows us to accept Hamlet's brutality towards Ophelia, his reaction to Polonius' death, his savage refusal to kill Claudius at prayer, and his Machiavellian delight in disposing of Rosencrantz and Guildenstern. Without the memory of the great soliloquies which preceded it, our impression of the closet scene would be vastly different.
>
> (235)

For Ornstein, our moral impression of Hamlet's character is of "an illusion within an illusion," Hamlet as he was before his shocks, as he is remembered by his schoolfellows, Ophelia, and himself. But if our vision of him is as unassailable as Ornstein says, what Hamlet does or says ceases to matter, let alone *how* he says it. It is impossible for me to imagine this ideal Hamlet speaking words that are going to be disregarded by his audience anyway. Robert G. Hunter's Hamlet, who sees himself as an agent of justice, is more plausible in reading these lines. In Hamlet's position, most of us, says Hunter, would be horribly remorseful, would pity ourselves for being forced into this position, and would try to get out of any consequences because we weren't responsible and were sorry. "Hamlet suffers no remorse, pities himself not a bit, and accepts his responsibility and the consequent necessity to answer for what he has done" (119). This Hamlet speaks the lines coldly, without arrogance, and with the confidence of what Hunter calls "his justified conviction that he is the scourge and minister of God" (118).

His confidence may indeed come from just and justified convictions about his task, but it may also result from a progressive coarsening of Hamlet's character. The latter is easier to convey in reading these lines than the former, though (as

Hunter and Ornstein rightly remind us) we, as audience, are eager to forgive Hamlet much.

How Polonius has been played earlier is another important consideration for this scene. In Richard Burton's *Hamlet,* Hume Cronyn played Polonius so sympathetically that the audience was shocked at his murder and never really forgave Hamlet for it.

"Thou turn'st mine eyes into my very soul"

At line 35 Hamlet shifts suddenly from the familiar in which he has been speaking to the dead Polonius back to the formal second person he always uses in addressing his mother:

> Leave wringing of your hands. Peace, sit you down
> And let me wring your heart
>
> (35–36)

Gertrude at first shows little consciousness of guilt in her reaction:

> What have I done that thou dar'st wag thy tongue
> In noise so rude against me?
>
> (40–41)

Hamlet's attack differs little in matter from that of his first soliloquy: he compares Claudius with old Hamlet and blames Gertrude for her choice, especially when she is at an age when "The heyday in the blood is tame" (70). Not even madness, but only a cozening devil (77–78) or "Rebellious hell" (83) could have tempted her. No young person can be blamed for passion when "compulsive ardor gives the charge" and "reason panders will" for a matron like Gertrude (86–89). The sole reference Hamlet makes to what he has learned since 1.2 is his calling Claudius "A murtherer and a villain" (97), and, though Gertrude may react to this, the text gives no further warrant than might be justified by her earlier line at 31: "As kill a king?" Hamlet may, in short, deliver these lines, as well as the "go not to my uncle's bed" speech (150–73), in the torment and sexual disgust he can show in the first soliloquy. He need not, like Olivier, stage a love scene with embraces and kisses on the mouth in order to make clear the Oedipal quality of his attempt to sever his mother from Claudius. The closet scene will retain a certain amount of this Oedipal quality even for greatly varying interpretations of the main character. As Clifford Leech has justly observed of the contribution Ernest Jones's *Hamlet and Oedipus* makes to *Hamlet* studies, "We need not . . . see the whole play in terms of the Oedipus complex in order to feel that Jones has made one of its components more graspable" (13).

One Hamlet, though, speaks these daggers to his mother as part of the revenge with which he has been charged. He may have forgotten or misunderstood his charge in thinking this a part of it; Maynard Mack thinks he has, when "he takes it upon himself to be his mother's conscience, though the ghost has warned that this is no fit task for him, and returns to repeat the warning" (522). It may be that "In separating Gertrude from Claudius and bringing her to repentance in thought and action," he is "indeed following the Ghost's instructions," as Fredson Bowers argues in "Hamlet's Fifth Soliloquy" (218–20). In any case, his manner will reflect his conviction that it is part of his task, despite or in addition to whatever Oedipal element the scene contains. For this Hamlet, what he knows about Claudius is precisely what has brought his thoughts in 1.2 from an internal, self-torturing conflict to action, as he tries to impel his mother spiritually and physically toward virtue and away from Claudius.

Little of this works rationally, and for one Hamlet, none of it does. For this Hamlet, the scene's parallel with Hamlet's interview with Ophelia is made more obvious by his madness and shifts back and forth from grim humor to uncontrolled rage. This Hamlet does not use the convention of the two miniature portraits of old Hamlet and Claudius, worn by Hamlet and Gertrude (the convention is at least as old as the Keans and Edwin Booth, according to Shattuck, 229). When he says,

"Look here upon this picture, and on this," he traces the features of his father and Claudius in the air. The scene with this Hamlet, instead of varying in pace and emotional temperature after Polonius's death and at the appearance and exit of the ghost, races hotly from Hamlet's entrance to its end, and even though the ghost is visible to us and speaking, we say with Gertrude, "Alas, he's mad," and know with her that the ghost is the "very coinage" of Hamlet's brain, a "bodiless creation ecstasy / Is very cunning in" (138–40). Although this unorthodox reaction seems inconsistent with our acceptance of an unsummoned ghost, independent of Hamlet, at the beginning of the play, there is psychological justification for it. Hamlet is, according to Clifford Leech, "the first character in an Elizabethan drama to doubt a ghost's veracity" (7), but once he has doubted, he opens the way for any subsequent appearance of the ghost as other than the confirmed and corroborated spirit of Hamlet's father, acting independently of his son's "weakness and melancholy."

The old questions—whether Gertrude is guilty of adultery and whether she had any part or knowledge of her husband's murder—are not resolved in this scene. In fact, except for Hamlet's apparently wild shot at line 30, they are not even taken up here. Hamlet belabors his mother with her choice of Claudius and with living with him. (When I write *here* I refer to the main substantive texts. The explicitness of Hamlet's accusations and Gertrude's denials in the First Quarto does not prove her innocence, as some have argued. All that is proved is the reconstructors' misunderstanding of a subtle scene.)

Gertrude accepts guilt and shame when she says that Hamlet turns her eyes into her very soul:

> And there I see such black and grainèd spots
> As will not leave their tinct.
>
> (91–92)

The stains Gertrude sees on her soul might well be the lust that Hamlet is taxing her with, or the ease with which she had been persuaded to marry Claudius, the fact of the marriage's technical incest, or something worse. Elsewhere Gertrude merely begs Hamlet to stop and tells him he has cleft her heart in twain. Rebecca Smith, in an article entitled "A Heart Cleft in Twain: The Dilemma of Shakespeare's Gertrude," reminds us that Gertrude makes no promises to Hamlet about avoiding Claudius's bed, and Smith invites us to look at a Gertrude somewhat different from that depicted by Kozintsev's, Olivier's or Richardson's films and many stage versions: "Gertrude's words and actions in Shakespeare's *Hamlet* create not the lusty, lascivious Gertrude that one generally sees in stage and film production, but a compliant, loving, unimaginative woman whose only concern is pleasing others" (206–7). Gertrude is problematic, but not complex; she is only problematic because we do not have enough information about her, and much of what we have is from others, "the ghost, Hamlet, and Claudius—all of whom see her literally and in quite heightened terms as a sexual *object*" (207). Smith sees her as innocent of the murder and of adultery (202–3), and conscious only of the "o'erhasty" nature of her remarriage. She does not modify her behavior after the closet scene and does not develop morally; "only her divided loyalties and her unhappiness intensify" (206).

Some conflict between the maternal and the marital is always going to be part of Gertrude's character, of course. But given that constant, there can be variation within each part: the maternal may be somewhat distant or uncomfortably, even sexually, close, while the marital may be overtly lusty or proper and staid.

"Do you see nothing there?"

At line 102 the ghost enters. The moment is psychologically charged, and it is Hamlet who has built this charge up. First Hamlet summons his father in description, then he uses a picture, and finally old Hamlet's very ghost appears. Thus the progression may be seen as Hamlet's unconscious conjuring of his father. The ghost may then appear either as the same spirit we have seen before, which sees the need to direct Hamlet back to his purpose, or solely as a manifestation of Hamlet's mind. Hamlet thinks he knows the ghost's purpose:

> Do you not come your tardy son to chide,
> That, lapsed in time and passion, lets go by
> Th' important acting of your dread command?
>
> (107-9)

And indeed, the ghost replies that it has come "to whet thy almost blunted purpose" (112). These words seem to imply that Hamlet's recent activities—the refusal to kill Claudius, the thrust through the arras, the conscience-stirring of his mother—have nothing to do with the task he has been set. But we do not have to set the ghost up as an interpreter of Hamlet's motives. Claudius is still alive, the called-for revenge means his death, and therefore the ghost has come to prompt Hamlet to action.

The ghost is not visible to Gertrude. Presumably it has the power of selective apparition. Gertrude's failure even to see the final and most potent reminder of her husband may be played as the failure of Hamlet to awaken her conscience and change her behavior toward Claudius. More than that, Gertrude's incapacity to see or recognize mortality is precisely what Hamlet sees and deplores early and late:

> QUEEN.   . . .
>   Thou know'st 'tis common. All that lives must die,
>   Passing through nature to eternity.
> HAMLET. Ay, madam, it is common.
>
> (1.2.72-74)

> HAMLET. [*Takes the skull.*] . . . . Now get you to my lady's
>   chamber, and tell her, let her paint an inch thick, to this
>   favor she must come.
>
> (5.1.180-82)

Gertrude here provides an example of the importance of the unseen—what a spectator cannot or will not see. Hamlet asks her if she sees nothing there. She replies: "Nothing at all; yet all that is I see" (133). Gertrude may not even look in the direction Hamlet indicates, so certain is she that there is nothing there. Hers is a material vision and a certain failure of imagination. It may result from a vicious nature, a merely sensual one, or the more benign and unimaginative Gertrude for whom Rebecca Smith argues.

". . . to draw toward an end with you"

Has Gertrude agreed to anything at the end of the scene? Hamlet tells her "go not to my uncle's bed," but she does not assent to this in any speech. Claire Bloom's Gertrude in fact looks most unwilling to agree; Kozintsev's, on the other hand, shrinks from Claudius after this point in the play. Gertrude's "What shall I do?" (181) is ambiguous: she may be meekly asking Hamlet for instructions, his "One word more, good lady"; but it is also possible that she asks what to do in despair of Hamlet's condition or over her own conflict in trying to please an angry son and an angry husband.

Hamlet bids her to keep silent

> That I essentially am not in madness,
> But mad in craft.
>
> (188–89)

Gertrude assures him only that she will not repeat what he has said. Her reply raises its own questions:

> Be thou assured, if words be made of breath,
> And breath of life, I have no life to breathe
> What thou hast said to me.
>
> (198–200)

This, too, is capable of more than one reading. She may have no life to breathe it because it describes too much of her own shame, or no life to breathe it because it is such frightening and desperate madness. Gertrude may be convinced that Hamlet is only "mad in craft," but she may also be speaking the plain truth as she sees it when she tells Claudius in the next scene that Hamlet is mad.

Hamlet begins to say good night 55 lines before the scene

ends, but pauses or returns to say something more. The pattern is repeated three times. Hamlet's first message is "go not to my uncle's bed." His second begins at 171:

> Once more, good night,
> And when you are desirous to be blest,
> I'll blessing beg of you. —For this same lord,
> I do repent; but heaven hath pleased it so,
> To punish me with this, and this with me,
> That I must be their scourge and minister.
> I will bestow him and will answer well
> The death I gave him.
>
> (171–78)

Burton's Hamlet begins to cry at this point, but it is not clear whether he is reacting to the end of a trying scene with his mother or whether he is softening his earlier words about Polonius and underscoring "I do repent." In any case he suddenly stops crying and is hard and scornful at "One word more, good lady" (181), then eases again at "I must to England" (201). Every Hamlet has to span broad dramatic scales in this scene, and Burton's interpretation has the desirable result of giving emphasis to all three of the matters that come quickly at the end of this scene: the prediction Hamlet makes about answering Polonius's death, his warning to his mother not to give him away, and his grim forecast of the destruction of Rosencrantz and Guildenstern. Needless to say, the changes of tone necessary in a rational Hamlet can be exaggerated in a mad one, who will emphasize the disparity between "For this same lord, I do repent" and "I'll lug the guts into the neighbor room" (213). There is warrant for Hamlet's weeping at the scene's end: Gertrude says in the next scene "'A weeps for what is done" (27). Finally, at 218, Hamlet says "Good night" for the fifth and last time.

Act Four

The play has now entered a catastrophic phase, and it is possible to see the rest of its movement in terms of deaths. The scenes customarily grouped as Act Four constitute the interval between the death of Polonius and the death of Ophelia; those of Act Five, the interval between the death of Ophelia and the death of Hamlet. Within the larger movement from the death of Polonius to that of Ophelia there are two groups of scenes. The first deals with Hamlet's departure and comprises the short scenes 4.1, 4.2, 4.3, and the appearance of Fortinbras leading to Hamlet's soliloquy in 4.4. The second group shows us Ophelia mad at the beginning (4.5) and tells us of Ophelia drowned at the end (4.7); the sequence is interrupted by the return of the two avengers (4.5 and 4.6). Laertes returns first, loudly; then Hamlet, more quietly, by report.

Scene One

While Claudius and Gertrude speak in this scene, they also leave much unsaid. Claudius asks "How does Hamlet?" and Gertrude's answer conceals Hamlet's madness-in-craft. Claudius hides his awareness that Hamlet is now clearly set on a bloody revenge; he would of course have to reveal his own guilt to Gertrude in order to tell her of his awareness of Hamlet's motive and intent. Claudius also conceals his own intent:

he had already resolved or has just resolved to order Hamlet's death. If, on the other hand, Gertrude and Claudius are co-conspirators, they must both know that Hamlet has the truth about his father's murder. But Gertrude as co-conspirator will still try to conceal from Claudius the extent of Hamlet's threat, while Claudius will hide his plan to make Hamlet's exile his death.

Claudius begins by imploring Gertrude to "translate" the meaning of her sighs and heaves into words. (Actress and reader's mind's eye have already translated Claudius's speech here into appropriate action for Gertrude.) Gertrude does not immediately answer directly: "Ah, mine own lord, what have I seen tonight!" (5). Gertrude echoes Ophelia's reaction to her interview with Hamlet, "O, woe is me T' have seen what I have seen, see what I see!" (3.1.160–61), but Ophelia saw very little by comparison. Gertrude tells Claudius that Hamlet is mad and has killed the "good old man" Polonius. The sequence of thoughts in Claudius's reaction is characteristic:

> O heavy deed!
> It had been so with us, had we been there.
> His liberty is full of threats to all,
> To you yourself, to us, to every one.
> Alas, how shall this bloody deed be answered?
> It will be laid to us.
>
> (12–17)

His reaction to the seriousness of the act is followed immediately by his thought for his own safety. Then, as if to justify that thought, he speaks of Hamlet's danger to Gertrude and to everyone as well as to himself. Then again he thinks of how Polonius's death will be received publicly.

The following lines change their effect depending on whether Claudius uses the *us*, *our*, and *we* to refer to himself (as in 13–15) or to himself and Gertrude:

> It will be laid to us, whose providence
> Should have kept short, restrained, and out of haunt
> This mad young man. But so much was our love
> We would not understand what was most fit,

> But, like the owner of a foul disease,
> To keep it from divulging, let it feed
> Even on the pith of life.
>   (17–23)

"But so much was our love," if it refers to Claudius's love for Hamlet, is an empty formula, but if it includes Gertrude—the love they both bear Hamlet—it rings truer. Referring to Claudius's love for Gertrude, it is a real explanation for Claudius's "delay" in reacting to the threat Hamlet poses for him.

One choice is between a Claudius isolated by this act, or one drawn closer to Gertrude by it. And the extent to which Gertrude tries to heed Hamlet's bidding in the previous scene affects Claudius's isolation. She tells him that Hamlet "weeps for what is done" (27). Is this invention, or a straightforward description of Hamlet during some part of the last scene? If invention, it may tend to increase the feeling we have that Gertrude is trying to obey Hamlet and distance Claudius. Kozintsev chose to underline his view of how these tensions are resolved by having Claudius and Gertrude exit this scene by climbing separate wings of a huge staircase, presumably on their way to separate sleeping arrangements.

Another choice is that between a Claudius who is beginning to unravel and one who is still in control. The former stresses the "come away" twice addressed to Gertrude, the hope that any harm from Polonius's death "may miss our name" (43), and the "discord and dismay" (45) that fills his soul. The latter has finally determined how to deal with Hamlet and now sends Rosencrantz and Guildenstern to find Polonius's body while he considers how to reconcile their "wisest friends" to the fact of his death.

Scene Two

Hamlet continues his antic disposition, though the main person who believed it is dead. If this is merely ineffectual fooling, it tends to make Hamlet's exile and destruction by Claudius look more likely to be successful, thus heightening suspense. But Hamlet's lines in this scene are susceptible of at least two other readings.

Hamlet may be trying to warn Rosencrantz and Guildenstern bluntly. He has already told us that he will "delve one yard below their mines / And blow them at the moon" (3.4.209–10) if they get in his way. Now he calls Rosencrantz a sponge "that soaks up the king's countenance, his rewards, his authorities" (15–16), and implies that he is a fool if he does not understand this speech (22–23).

Another, perhaps complementary, view of Hamlet's lines here is that of Maurice Charney, who considers them to be examples of Hamlet's "witty style," which is mostly, but not exclusively, associated with Hamlet's supposed madness. Charney sees Hamlet's use of the witty style in 4.2 and 4.3 as emphasizing "an ironic contrast between Hamlet's present status"—virtual house arrest—"and his absolute self-assurance. With colloquial mockery, he taunts the king and his court, whose only defense is to pretend not to understand" (292). Charney's Hamlet is one who has confidently taken control of the action since 3.2, and who, even in the grasp of Claudius, seems confident of his eventual escape.

Scene Three

This scene gives Hamlet an opportunity to aim his jests directly at Claudius, and it allows Claudius to tell us that he has ordered Hamlet's death. Essentially it is a mortal confrontation between the two, but Claudius does not tell us of the stakes on his side until the very end of the scene.

In the Second Quarto scene, Claudius speaks to the "*two or three*" with whom he has entered. The lack of this stage direction in the Folio makes of his first speech a soliloquy and thus changes it drastically. The Quarto direction suggests that

Claudius is following his own directions in 4.1 to "call up our wisest friends / And let them know both what we mean to do / And what's untimely done" (4.1.38–40):

> I have sent to seek him and to find the body.
> How dangerous is it that this man goes loose!
> Yet must not we put the strong law on him;
> He's loved of the distracted multitude . . . .
>   To bear all smooth and even,
> This sudden sending him away must seem
> Deliberate pause. Diseases desperate grown
> By desperate appliance are relieved,
> Or not at all.
>
>   (1–4, 7–11)

The decisive Claudius has already gathered the counselors who may save his reputation; he has acted to gather in Hamlet and to begin to deal with Polonius's remains. He reminds these counselors that Hamlet's act is confirmation of the danger he predicted in 3.1 and 3.3. Hamlet himself thus justifies the speedy exile of which everyone knows, and by implication, the further desperate measure of which they do not know, Hamlet's execution abroad. But there is another Claudius possible in these lines, one whose nerve is broken. He no longer acts by his own sovereign authority but seeks the support of others for his decisions. One of these decisions is a request that another king take the step Claudius is afraid to take himself.

Rosencrantz enters, and then Hamlet, who is now under guard. In the following exchanges, Hamlet adumbrates themes that will occupy his thoughts for the rest of the play. His topics are the inevitability of death; the commonality of death for the great and the small, king and beggar alike; and the decay of the body after death.

Does he speak calmly or frenetically? If calmly, he has already begun to come to that cool resignation he shows in the last scene of the play (Hamlet has only three more scenes), and his behavior gives the lie to Claudius's attempt to show the others how mad he is: "Alas, alas!" says Claudius (26), echoing Gertrude's "Alas, he's mad" (3.4.106). If he speaks frenetically, we will see a contrast later when he makes these same observa-

tions about kings and worms more calmly in 5.1, further gener-
alized to Alexander, Caesar, and my Lady Worm, or talks of the
readiness for death being all that is important, in 5.2. Modern
Hamlets frequently play the scene calmly (Olivier, Burton, Jacobi), but if Claudius is played so too, some of the scene's possibilities for tension are lost: Hamlet's calmness seems to call
for nerves and wrath from Claudius, while any frenzy on
Hamlet's part can cool and confirm the king.

In answer to the king's question about Polonius's body,
Hamlet tells Claudius to go to hell. This fact, if it were simply
so, would simplify any reading of Hamlet's lines: we have
clearly a courageous young man, not afraid to beard his powerful uncle, even when under guard and in danger of death. But
Hamlet does not simply tell Claudius to go to hell; he uses a
euphemism, "th' other place," and he immediately afterwards
tells Claudius what he wants to know.

Claudius tells Hamlet he is bound for England, and
Hamlet bids farewell by calling Claudius "dear mother" (48).

> KING. Thy loving father, Hamlet.
> HAMLET. My mother—father and mother is man and wife,
> man and wife is one flesh, and so, my mother. Come,
> for England!
>
> (49–52)

During this speech Olivier works his open hands as if he
would strangle Claudius, but then weakly drifts into the last
line. The gesture is a perhaps gratuitous reminder that the
Oedipal Hamlet is still restrained from revenge by more than
guards. But the psychologically unblocked Hamlet has other
reasons for not having killed Claudius to this point: a wish to
damn him (3.3), the wrong person behind the arras (3.4), and
guards (4.3).

Left alone, the king announces that he has commanded the
English king to kill Hamlet:

> Do it, England,
> For like the hectic in my blood he rages,
> And thou must cure me
>
> (64–66)

Patrick Stewart's Claudius speaks the line so imploringly we
are led to ask whether in fact the English king would so readily
have killed a Danish prince as he did Rosencrantz and Guildenstern. Stewart's Claudius is only a little way along toward a
reading of the character as Hamlet sees him: a man unfit to be
king, unworthy of respect, and one who does not understand
how princes act (Norway, Fortinbras, and England). The reader
always feels the pressure of this Claudius beneath the successful schemer and cool head of state. It can be argued that
none of Claudius's schemes is actually successful, except his
last one, and that is so badly botched that it destroys not only
its intended victim, Hamlet, but also the queen, Laertes, and
Claudius himself.

Scene Four

Another way to look at the concluding movements of the
play, besides that from death to death, is to see the final movement beginning here, with the entry of the first avenger, Fortinbras. In 4.4. 4.5, and 4.6 all three avengers reenter the play,
though Fortinbras is immediately sent off again, not to return
until the last scene, and Hamlet's presence is only reported for
two scenes, while Laertes' counter-revenge plot is developed.
This scene consists of the appearance of Fortinbras, on his way
to conquer a small part of Poland, and the last soliloquy of
Hamlet, occasioned by seeing the martial preparations of Fortinbras. In the Folio the scene ends after the exit of Fortinbras
and his attendants; there is no soliloquy and Hamlet does not
appear. The Quarto version preserves one of Hamlet's greatest
speeches and thereby makes a contrast between the Hamlet
before his departure for England, still chiding himself for inaction, and the serener Hamlet after his return. The Folio version
can be defended on structural grounds. Hamlet's absence from
the scene means that his departure has already occurred and

therefore does not interrupt the sequence: Fortinbras's entry—
Laertes' return—Hamlet's return.

This is our first view of Fortinbras. His few lines here and
in 5.2, together with what others say of him, must make up a
characterization. Horatio says he is "Of unimprovèd mettle hot
and full" (1.1.96) and Hamlet calls him "a delicate and tender
prince" (4.4.48). Thus we have some scope to create our Fortinbras, and our view of him will depend to some extent on our
view of Hamlet, since the two are destined to be compared,
from their similar situations at the first mention of them in 1.1
until Fortinbras buries Hamlet in 5.2. The comparison is made
explicit by Hamlet himself here in 4.4.

Hamlet does not meet Fortinbras, but sees his army, and
asking, discovers that the Norwegians "go to gain a little patch
of ground / That hath in it no profit but the name" (17–18).
This revelation gives rise to Hamlet's soliloquy, as the player's
weeping for Hecuba gives rise to the first soliloquy in which he
accuses himself of cowardice. Hamlet's frequent comparisons
of himself to other men move gradually toward those objects
most like himself in fortune and purpose: he compares himself
to Hercules (1.1.152), to himself in the past (1.5.97ff. and
2.2.292ff.), to the player (2.2.535), to other men in honesty
(3.1.122), to Horatio (3.2.59), to Fortinbras (4.4.46), and finally
to Laertes (5.2.77ff.).

The tone of this soliloquy is far less passionate and more
philosophical than that of the "rogue and peasant slave"
speech. There is one exclamation at the beginning and another
at the end (where the earlier speech has eight), and the thought
moves with an appearance of rational progression from a general question and answer about man's purpose toward how it
has been defeated in the particular case of Hamlet (bestial oblivion or cowardly scruples). Then it moves to the "exhorting"
example of Fortinbras and his army, who dare all for a straw, and
back to Hamlet, whose reasons for action are much greater.
Finally it concludes with a resolution to think bloody thoughts.

It is a puzzling speech in many ways, and not merely for
those who follow Werder and G. B. Harrison (108–9) in seeing

Hamlet as a courageous man of action thwarted only by external causes. Looking back at the events of Act Three alone, we can only consider the charge of "bestial oblivion" as valid if we adopt the point of view of the ghost. Hamlet has arranged and brought off the play to assure himself the ghost has not abused him in order to damn him (is this a "craven scruple"?), has determined not to stab Claudius in the back in circumstances that look like sending him to heaven (a diabolical scruple perhaps—and perhaps a craven one), has stabbed Polonius with the apparent misapprehension that he *was* killing Claudius (misses do not count for the ghost, understandably, but he speaks of Hamlet's "almost blunted purpose" to a man with a bloody sword still in hand), and he has made Gertrude look into her soul and admit that she sees "black and grainèd spots" there.

One Hamlet, at least, has adopted the ghost's view. The ghost ordered Hamlet not to let "the royal bed of Denmark be / A couch for luxury and damned incest" (1.5.82–83), but Hamlet *has* allowed precisely this so far, and not having dealt with those who pollute Denmark, he now identifies himself with them and their bestial nature. Thus "a beast that wants discourse of reason / Would have mourned longer" (1.2.150–51), spoken of his mother, is now echoed in his words about himself:

> What is a man,
> If his chief good and market of his time
> Be but to sleep and feed? A beast, no more.
> Sure he that made us with such large discourse,
> Looking before and after, gave us not
> That capability and godlike reason
> To fust in us unused. Now, whether it be
> Bestial oblivion
>
> (33–40)

This Hamlet, whose self-disgust has been evident since his first words in soliloquy, puts himself among the feeding, sleeping, and rutting beasts. This Hamlet is not impressed with Fortinbras's enterprise; though it is an example to spur him, it is an example "gross as earth" and Fortinbras himself "puffed" with ambition, while the soldiers go to their deaths "for a fantasy."

But another Hamlet shows us here that his examples and models have indeed moved from players to soldiers, whose enterprise, despite its futility, is both honorable and a "great argument." Their leader, moreover, is puffed up, but with *divine* ambition:

> Witness this army of such mass and charge,
> Led by a delicate and tender prince,
> Whose spirit, with divine ambition puffed,
> Makes mouths at the invisible event,
> Exposing what is mortal and unsure
> To all that fortune, death, and danger dare,
> Even for an eggshell. Rightly to be great
> Is not to stir without great argument,
> But greatly to find quarrel in a straw
> When honor's at the stake. How stand I then,
>   . . . while to my shame I see
> The imminent death of twenty thousand men
> That for a fantasy and trick of fame
> Go to their graves like beds, fight for a plot
> Whereon the numbers cannot try the cause,
> Which is not tomb enough and continent
> To hide the slain?
>
> (47–56, 59–65)

For this Hamlet, a memorable example of ready and untheatric courage is compressed in the line "Go to their graves like beds." (It seems to have been the line that most impressed George Bernard Shaw about the soliloquy—Shaw 82, 84.) Something like that unhesitating courage will spur his boarding of the pirate ship and let him find the most important virtue in readiness.

For either Hamlet, the logic of the soliloquy is compelling, even though we may see it as specious. No insistence that he is not cowardly, has not failed to act, will convince the despairing and self-loathing Hamlet. Only his desperation will explain how this Hamlet manages to destroy Rosencrantz and Guildenstern, lead the fight against the pirates, and engineer his own return to Denmark. Nor will the newly martial Hamlet be

slowed by criticisms that the sentiment, "Rightly to be great /
Is not to stir without great argument," is crippled, if not contradicted, by "But greatly to find quarrel in a straw / When
honor's at the stake."

Scenes Five, Six, and Seven

This section is sometimes played continuously with the
middle scene cut (thus Evans's G. I. *Hamlet* and Burton's production in 1964), but 4.6 gives us important information
and makes a necessary separation between the two Laertes-
Ophelia scenes, which differ in tone: the first is a scene of madness, passion, and turmoil, while the last is one of death and
cold-blooded plans for murder. Moreover there is a rhythm in
the first and last scenes repeated in the whole of the three-
scene sequence: each has two or three people engaged in conversation and suddenly interrupted by an unexpected entry or
return.

Ophelia's Madness

Scene Five begins with Gertrude's refusal to see Ophelia,
which is only partly explained by the queen's soliloquy at 17.
Ophelia's behavior and speech are described by a Gentleman,
who also comments on how hearers take her ravings:

> [she] speaks things in doubt
> That carry but half sense. Her speech is nothing,
> Yet the unshapèd use of it doth move
> The hearers to collection; they aim at it,
> And botch the words up fit to their own thoughts,
> Which, as her winks and nods and gestures yield them,
> Indeed would make one think there might be thought,
> Though nothing sure. . . . .

(6–13)

This is indeed a description of what we do with Ophelia's lines, as readers, directors, and actresses.

In the Second Quarto, Horatio persuades the Queen to see Ophelia by arguing that she "may strew / Dangerous conjectures in ill-breeding minds" (14–15); the Queen convinces herself in the Folio. Horatio's function here at court, as well as his concern here, are puzzling, unless he is merely concerned with his friend's good name, but that Ophelia could hurt Hamlet's reputation seems unlikely. She seems to know none of the facts about her father's death; see, for example, line 184.

Gertrude, convinced she must see Ophelia, speaks in soliloquy:

> To my sick soul (as sin's true nature is)
> Each toy seems prologue to some great amiss.
> So full of artless jealousy is guilt
> It spills itself in fearing to be spilt.
>   (17–20)

These lines are equivocal, referring as they might to guilt felt for her son's sake at Polonius's death or at the way she and Claudius have handled it (see lines 83–84) or to deeper guilts at her lust (which Ophelia's innocence emphasizes by contrast) or adultery or complicity in murder. Distinctions among these cannot easily be made in acting.

Ophelia enters asking "Where is the beauteous majesty of Denmark?" (21), a sarcastic line as Lalla Ward reads it in the BBC *Hamlet*. T. J. B. Spencer suggests other possibilities (311–12): "This may mean merely 'Where is the Queen?' or possibly 'Where has your queenly beauty gone?' (addressed to the Queen, who, now conscience-ridden, may be looking very different from the happy woman of the scenes up to 3.4)." Ophelia sings most of her part in this scene, enabling the play to use some of the complex appeal of songs (only *Hamlet, Othello,* and *Lear* among the tragedies have more than a single song, and half the tragedies have none). We expect the mad to sing. Ophelia can sing what she could not say, just as she can say, mad, what she would not or could not say, sane. She sings about the "tumbling" of a maid, and though she says she will end the song without an oath, swears "By Cock" that young men are to blame that they "will do't if they come to't" (60–61). It is possible to exaggerate this element in Ophelia's madness, as Marianne Faithfull did in Richardson's *Hamlet*—but then her Ophelia had been played as a wanton throughout. There is no bawdry in Ophelia's scene with Laertes, and yet the suggestiveness of the first part of the scene is often extended, as when Lalla Ward's Ophelia kisses Laertes on the mouth, open-mouthed, at her entrance at 154. Jean Simmons's Ophelia is fairly restrained: she makes eyes at Horatio and shows a good deal of décolletage, but she is prim with Laertes and her Valentine song is obscured by business and almost inaudible, as if Olivier wishes to remove even the barest suggestion that his Hamlet might have coupled with Ophelia, even in the repressed depths of her mind. Kozintsev's Ophelia is chaste and angelic in the midst of her ballads, above the sensuality of her royal hosts.

Ophelia's songs are of love and death, pointing to the causes of her madness. These have been Hamlet's topics also, and as with Hamlet, the grief for the dead father is simple and innocent but the love with which it is linked is shameful and painful. Ophelia's remarks, as well as her songs, can be made apposite—that is, those to whom she addresses a remark can be expected to "botch the words up fit to their own thoughts," especially if they have guilty consciences. Thus her "Lord, we know what we are, but know not what we may be" (43–44), if not spoken of her own situation in a lucid moment (Jean Simmons's Ophelia) but to Gertrude or Claudius, will make either of them quail.

At her first exit Ophelia speaks directly of her father:

> I hope all will be well. We must be patient, but I cannot choose but weep to think they would lay him i' th' cold ground. My brother shall know of it; and so I thank you for your good counsel. Come, my coach! Good night, ladies, good night. Sweet ladies, good night, good night. (68–73)

When she speaks of patience and all being well, she may, like Lear with the dead Cordelia, pathetically believe Polonius will recover. Or the comment may refer to Polonius's soul, in which case the patience looks toward judgment and the whole reinforces the *respice finem* that is a favorite theme of Hamlet's also. "My brother shall know of it," spoken in anger, reminds us that Ophelia too is a kind of revenger. Is she sincere when she thanks them for their "good counsel"? Lalla Ward is sarcastic here; Jean Simmons merely sweet.

We must be prepared to admit that Ophelia's madness can be funny. The fact that all those onstage are saddened by her behavior does not mean that the groundling represented in a small way in each of us gentle readers cannot be amused. She can be comic here when she asks for her coach. The leave-taking at 72–74 may be addressed to the empty air, but can also be a parallel of something we have already seen: "Good night, ladies [*to Horatio and Claudius*], good night [*to Gertrude*]. Sweet ladies, good night [*to Horatio and Claudius*], good night [*to Gertrude*]." We see the mad person here as *contrary,* but the scene also echoes Hamlet's leave-taking of Claudius in 4.3, where he calls him *mother.*

Claudius speaks after Ophelia's exit, assigning the cause of her madness wholly to grief over her father's death. He does not acknowledge that love for Hamlet may be a factor, as he did not acknowledge that their "o'erhasty marriage" might have been part of the cause of Hamlet's disturbance. Claudius lists the "sorrows" that have come in battalions: Polonius's death, Hamlet's removal, the people's unrest, Ophelia's madness, Laertes' dangerous return. Of these Claudius is responsible only for sending Hamlet away, though he admits, in regard to Polonius's burial, that they "have done but greenly / In hugger-mugger to inter him" (83–84). The strong Claudius is disturbed at the loss of control he feels, and at being blamed for what he did not do; he shows Shakespeare's insight into the petulant sensitivity of the guilty about false blame. This Claudius fears the threat to the crown, and commiserates with Gertrude. The weaker Claudius is not so much commiserating as throwing himself on Gertrude's support and soothing. He too resents the false blame—petulantly—but fears the personal danger most.

Laertes' Return

The metaphor used by the messenger who announces
Laertes' return enables us to see the mob without having to
bring it onstage. The image suggests both unstoppability and
going beyond proper bounds:

> The ocean, overpeering of his list,
> Eats not the flats with more impiteous haste
> Than young Laertes', in a riotous head,
> O'erbears your officers.
>
> (99–102)

The scene is capable of a good deal of irony, since a conservative myth is being invoked to denounce a challenge to an
upstart king:

> as the world were now but to begin,
> Antiquity forgot, custom not known,
> The ratifiers and props of every word,
> They cry, 'Choose we!'
>
> (103–6)

Suddenly Claudius's doubtful accession is forgotten; in the
messenger's words it is as if he had become king by ordinary
and rightful succession instead of by a possibly self-ratified
preemptive marriage of the widowed queen, having widowed
her himself. Events move so fast here that our audience sympathy may be shifted without our being aware of it. If the mob
constitutes a real threat, if Laertes is a formidable opponent,
and if Claudius faces him coolly and courageously, then we
may be on the king's side. Coleridge says his lines about di-
vinity hedging a king are proof "as indeed all else is, that
Shakespeare never intended us to see the king with Hamlet's
eyes, tho', I suspect, the managers have long done so" (1:34).
But in this century more managers see Claudius with Coleridge's eyes, and make this the king's shining moment. Yet
Claudius does not have to face the "riotous head" that stays
outside and is never heard from again after Laertes' entrance.
Claudius faces only Laertes, and in fact is shielded from him at
first by Gertrude, who defies the mob ("O, this is counter, you

false Danish dogs!") and tries to calm Laertes. Laertes will not
be calmed immediately:

> That drop of blood that's calm proclaims me bastard,
> Cries cuckold to my father, brands the harlot
> Even here between the chaste unsmirchèd brows
> Of my true mother.
>
> (117–20)

We note in passing that Laertes' image couples revenge for a
dead father with shameful love, and further that Laertes' manner of desperate passion can easily be played so as to enervate
the character and defuse his threat:

> To hell allegiance, vows to the blackest devil!
> Conscience and grace to the profoundest pit!
> I dare damnation.
>
> (131–33)

Laertes is full of superlatives and absolutes. He is "too hot and
choleric, and somewhat rhodomontade," according to Hazlitt
(237). He opposes all the world's will, and is ready to die for his
father's friends as well as be damned in revenge on his father's
enemies. Even a shaky Claudius manages to quiet him,
though, by assuring him that no one will stop him. Claudius's
catechizing of Laertes (Who will stop you? Will you kill both
friend and foe? Will you know Polonius's enemies?) leads up to
the assurance that Claudius is guiltless of Polonius's death. Beyond this Claudius cannot go with Gertrude present. Later,
having quieted Laertes with the help of Gertrude, he will proceed to plot against her son. But now the scene's interrupter is
himself interrupted as Ophelia reenters at 153. Ophelia's madness supplies another motive for revenge: "By heaven, thy
madness shall be paid by weight" (156); it is an effect of Polonius's death but also a cause of revenge itself, and moreover
seen as a kind of death:

> O heavens, is't possible a young maid's wits
> Should be as mortal as an old man's life?
>
> (159–60)

Now that Laertes and Ophelia are together it is easier to see
them as two halves of a grieved child, reflecting and exaggerat-

ing, while Hamlet is offstage, the different sides of *his* grief and desire for revenge. Ophelia's songs and fragmentary remarks express the sorrow and helplessness of her grief: "He is dead and gone. . . . to think they would lay him i' th' cold ground. . . . And will 'a not come again? No, no, he is dead. . . . He never will come again" (29, 69–70, 188, 190, 192). The sorrow and futility remind us of that aspect of Hamlet's reaction to his father's death—that sense of a place in the memory painful whenever touched:

> Heaven and earth,
> Must I remember?
>
> (1.2.142–43)

But Ophelia also, in one reading of her part, reflects Hamlet's wit and savage candor in calling vice and foolishness by their right names. This Ophelia's remarks are carefully aimed and take effect while to those untouched they seem to be about her songs, herself, or nothing: "Lord, we know what we are, but know not what we may be. . . . I thank you for your good counsel. . . . It is the false steward, that stole his master's daughter. . . . God 'a' mercy on his soul! And of all Christian souls, I pray God" (43–44, 70–71, 171–72, 197–98). For Claudius, she has fennel for flattery and columbines for ingratitude. She and Gertrude must wear their rue with a difference: for Ophelia it is sorrow for a dead father; for Gertrude it *ought* to be sorrow for a dead husband, and repentance. Gertrude is also given a daisy (infidelity); there are no more violets (faithfulness). Not all Ophelias read their lines with the same edge, but the character may do much, protected by genuine madness. Finally, she either commits suicide (which Hamlet had considered) or else receives death without a great struggle, as if it were a release (as Hamlet had talked of it in the "To be or not to be" soliloquy).

Laertes gives us the other half of grief, or perhaps the other extreme—ranting in anger, ready for blood, daring damnation. He recalls for us the ranting at the end of Act Two, where Hamlet, prompted to his revenge by heaven and hell, is unpacking his heart with words and "cursing like a very drab" (2.2.57off.). Hamlet, too, is resolute, but has his revenge turned aside (3.3) and directed against the wrong object (3.4). Each of the revengers is deflected at some point from the rightful object or direct acting of his revenge. Hamlet mistakes Claudius for a penitent and Polonius for Claudius; Laertes thinks Claudius responsible for Polonius's death at first, but fails to kill him. Fortinbras is talked into diverting his action against Denmark toward Poland. Hamlet and Fortinbras almost fall into their ultimate revenges. Laertes seems to be more direct, but he has allowed himself to be talked into an unnecessary plot when the direct approach ("tell him to his teeth, 'Thus diddest thou'"—4.7.55–56) would have been honorable.

Claudius advises Laertes to "Make choice of whom your wisest friends you will" to hear the facts of Polonius's death and acquit the king of blame (199–209). Claudius may assume Laertes will choose some of the same "wisest friends" he has briefed immediately after Polonius's death (4.1.38). No Claudius will have qualms about sacrificing Hamlet's memory to his own safety, and at this point Claudius believes Hamlet dead.

Hamlet's Return

Scene Six makes a necessary separation in a sequence between Claudius and Laertes. 4.5, with Gertrude present, shows Laertes, heated and passionate, vowing what heroic, world- and heaven-daring things he will do to avenge his father. With Gertrude necessarily absent, 4.7 shows Laertes coolly planning what scheming tricks he will use to kill Hamlet. The passion of Ophelia and Laertes controls the first scene, Claudius's policy the last.

The scene also enables us to hear a description of the pirate episode that Hamlet does not provide otherwise. Olivier could not resist showing it to us in his film. Kozintsev resisted, though he included one scene of Hamlet on shipboard.

> Ere we were two days old at sea, a pirate of very warlike
> appointment gave us chase. Finding ourselves too slow of
> sail, we put on a compelled valor, and in the grapple I
> boarded them. On the instant they got clear of our ship; so I
> alone became their prisoner.
>
> (15–20)

Shakespeare needed a way to get Hamlet back to Denmark, but
why did he invent this particular episode, not in the sources?
Geoffrey Bullough speculates, in *Narrative and Dramatic Sources
of Shakespeare*, that it was "an obvious means of proving
Hamlet's gallantry, short-circuiting the journey to England,
and linking his northern tale" with romances like Sidney's *Arcadia*, which Shakespeare knew well (47). Bullough prints an
extract from the *Arcadia* describing a pirate fight as an analogue
to the *Hamlet* incident. That the scene shows Hamlet's gallantry begs a question we have already examined in 4.4, but
whether we perform this offstage drama with an unhesita-
tingly courageous Hamlet or a desperate one (stressing the
"compelled valor" of his own account), Hamlet's return is sig-
nalled with extraordinary action and escape from great danger.

By means of the letter to Horatio, we learn of Hamlet's return as soon as the first person in Denmark knows, and, once
again, the audience's interests are identified with Horatio's.

As 4.7 begins, Claudius and Laertes are in the midst of
talk, and the scene consists mostly of their conversation, controlled by Claudius, who does most of the talking. Paralleling
4.5, this scene also has two surprising interruptions, but here
the first announces that one who was thought dead is alive,
and the second that one who was thought living is now dead.
The scene ends with Laertes motivated for revenge by two
deaths and Hamlet, twice-announced, about to return to the
play's action.

At the scene's opening Claudius has already convinced
Laertes that Hamlet killed Polonius and threatened the king as
well. The speech giving the scene's greatest latitude of interpretation to Claudius is that in which he answers Laertes'

question why he "proceeded not against these feats / So crime-
ful and so capital in nature" (6–7). Laertes is speaking of a public trial, because although he has dared damnation and later
will swear his willingness to cut Hamlet's throat in church, at
least one Laertes is really very conventional. In fact, the more
bravado he shows in 4.5, the more conventional and more
slavish in falling in with Claudius's plan he is likely to be here.
He may be played as somewhat more ominously quiet in the
previous scene (not an easy interpretation), and scornful of
Claudius's cowardice here. The part has less scope than any
other of the major roles because Laertes shows us only one
aspect of the revenger, while Hamlet shows so many.

Perhaps responding to a sneer from Laertes, Claudius begins by deprecating the apparent strength of his restraints:

> O, for two special reasons,
> Which may to you perhaps seem much unsinewed,
> But yet to me they're strong. The queen his mother
> Lives almost by his looks, and for myself—
> My virtue or my plague, be it either which—
> She is so conjunctive to my life and soul
> That, as the star moves not but in his sphere,
> I could not but by her. The other motive
> Why to a public count I might not go
> Is the great love the general gender bear him
>
> (9–18)

One Claudius, at least, speaks nothing but the truth here. This
Claudius loves Gertrude, after his fashion, and puts special
stress in soliloquy on his queen as one of the reasons for which
he killed (3.3.54–55). As for the people's love of Hamlet, we
have the king's words at 4.3.4. But another Claudius never
speaks the truth except for policy, and here he appeals to
Laertes' familial feelings by referring to love for Gertrude, and
he flatters Laertes indirectly by referring to the crowd's love for
Hamlet; Laertes knows that the prince is not the only one loved
by the people.

Laertes thinks himself unrevenged as long as Hamlet is
alive. Claudius is about to tell him that Hamlet is not alive, and
how he disposed of him, when a messenger enters announc-

ing letters from Hamlet. Since we already know of his safe return, no surprise prevents us from studying Claudius's reaction. One Claudius is rattled by the news:

> What should this mean? Are all the rest come back?
> Or is it some abuse, and no such thing?
>
> (48–49)

> Can you devise me?
>
> (52)

> If it be so, Laertes,
> (As how should it be so? how otherwise?)
>
> (56–57)

Even when his composure returns he comes up with a plan
that does *not* have the safety and sureness he talks of (63–67)
but which is in fact desperate, dangerous, and fated to go awry
in both its parts of swordplay and poison. But most modern
productions play Claudius as quick to recover from the shock
of Hamlet's return and resourceful in the cunning of his
scheme.

Claudius's scheme takes some seventy lines to develop.
Justifying Ophelia's giving him fennel for flattery, he begins by
flattering Laertes:

> KING.   It falls right.
> You have been talked of since your travel much,
> And that in Hamlet's hearing, for a quality
> Wherein they say you shine. Your sum of parts
> Did not together pluck such envy from him
> As did that one, and that, in my regard,
> Of the unworthiest siege.
> LAERTES.   What part is that, my lord?
>
> (69–75)

But Laertes does not get the answer to his question (which may
be disingenuous) for another two dozen lines, until Claudius
has actually introduced into his speech a character to report on
Laertes' skill, praised *him* outrageously, and let Laertes guess
who it is and praise him as well. This curiously slow dialogue
is shortened in the Folio, but even the cutting is done oddly,
going from "And call it accident" (67) to the beginning of the
speech about the Norman (80). During all of this Claudius tells

Laertes what might conduce him to agree with the plot (Laertes is by report a better swordsman than any in France; Hamlet was envious of his swordsmanship and eager to challenge him) and much that can hardly help (Claudius himself does not think swordsmanship a very worthy accomplishment; the Norman is a wondrous horseman). No recent production leaves in the whole of the business about Lamord (or Lamond, as in the Folio—either name is suggestive), or even mentions his name. More cuts were made in this (almost a fifth of the lines) than in any other scene in even the longest and most faithful production I have referred to, the BBC *Hamlet*.

Laertes fails to get Claudius's drift even after the long story about the Norman and about Hamlet's envy, which is the note the speech begins and ends on (73 and 102). Why does Laertes not see that Claudius wishes to suggest something more than a brother daring a brother to gentle exercise and proof of arms, or a straight duel with unbated swords? Or does he see and want to make Claudius *say* it rather than anticipating him? Once he understands the plot, Laertes is apt enough in suggesting a refinement, but before that point Claudius has been working hard (as he notes himself at 191). He has flattered Laertes by direct praise, by the reports of others and of the Norman in particular, and by Hamlet's twice-mentioned envy. He has piqued Laertes by asking whether his sorrow is real, and piqued him further by asking what he would do to avenge his father. A Laertes who is very young or very noble has to be brought a long way to become a junior partner in murderous policy, and the very length of seemingly unpertinent speeches here helps the plausibility of that movement. Claudius may go too far when he asks whether Polonius was dear to Laertes or whether he is "like the painting of a sorrow": while Laertes' "Why ask you this?" can be more puzzlement at where all this is going, Laertes may also have Claudius by the throat, so that the next speech is an apology:

> Not that I think you did not love your father,
> But that I know love is begun by time,
> And that I see, in passages of proof,
> Time qualifies the spark and fire of it.

> There lives within the very flame of love
> A kind of wick or snuff that will abate it,
> And nothing is at a like goodness still,
> For goodness, growing to a plurisy,
> Dies in his own too-much. That we would do
> We should do when we would, for this 'would' changes,
> And hath abatements and delays as many
> As there are tongues, are hands, are accidents,
> And then this 'should' is like a spendthrift sigh,
> That hurts by easing
>
> (109–22)

Whether in apology or not, Claudius comments unwittingly on Gertrude's abated love for her previous husband and Hamlet's delayed revenge. The speech, like the mad sorrow of Ophelia, the mad rage of Laertes, and the whole counter-revenge plot, keeps Hamlet's concerns before the audience's attention while he is absent.

Claudius finally presents his plan to Laertes at 130–38. It uses Hamlet's generosity and freedom from contrivance to kill him. Laertes adds a malicious refinement and Claudius a "back or second" to the plan. For a moment there was the possibility of straightforward shedding of blood, even though made possible by a subterfuge, but no one in the play except Polonius and Ophelia will be allowed to die other than by poison.

Ophelia's Death

Gertrude enters at 162 and, about to announce Ophelia's death near the end of 4.7, uses an image similar to but less warlike than the one Claudius used to comment on her madness near the beginning of 4.5.

> One woe doth tread upon another's heel,
> So fast they follow.
>
> (162–63)

Gertrude says "Your sister's drowned, Laertes" (163)—one of the least adorned announcements of a death in Shakespeare. Laertes' "Drowned! O, where?" introduces the willow speech, Gertrude's famous set speech, but his is a difficult line to make believable. T. J. B. Spencer suggests it is "a numbed reaction to the deeply felt calamity. Or Laertes may speak as if about to run to her" (330).

However he asks, his answer is a picture drawn in the mind's eye by Gertrude, who cannot be imagined as actually having been present at the drowning, but whose description we accept as necessarily right. Of course, Gertrude may possibly be inventing, to cover up the suicide suggested by clown and priest in the next scene. For the audience to see this there would need to be some wordless communication between Gertrude and Claudius while Laertes was distracted with the first news of Ophelia's death. But more frequently Gertrude delivers the speech as a description in the convention of circumstantial accounts of scenes the messenger could not have witnessed (cf. Hotspur's account of the encounter between Mortimer and Owen Glendower in *1 Henry IV*). Just as the imagery of Ophelia's songs had united ideas of sex and death, so does the description of her own death. She makes garlands of, among other flowers, "long purples, / That liberal shepherds give a grosser name, / But our cold maids do dead men's fingers call them" (168–70). The purples, with their ambiguous resemblance to male genitalia and dead men's fingers, create a picture within a picture, another emblem of the whole play, beautiful but sometimes crude, frequently mysterious, and always subtly dependent on the eye of the beholder for meaning. Ophelia's death is described as an equivocal triumph: she returns to nature with nature's flowers forming a crown and "trophies," though it is an "envious sliver" of the willow she is decking that precipitates her death. The water seems for a while her native element when she floats "mermaid-like" but eventually becomes "muddy death."

Laertes receives the news with an unspoken "speech o' fire, that fain would blaze," but for his tears. He is ashamed of the tears and calls them folly, but by saying, "When these are gone, / The woman will be out" (187–88), he reminds us, as the presence of both brother and sister onstage did, of the two halves of grief. Laertes exits, followed by Gertrude and Claudius, who fears the rekindling of Laertes' rage.

Act Five

Scene One

This moderately long scene (only 2.2, 5.2, and 3.2 are longer) is a series of six conversations, each forty to sixty lines in length. The two clowns hold the stage at the beginning. Then Horatio and Hamlet converse, then Hamlet and the First Clown, then Hamlet and Horatio again. Ophelia's funeral procession enters, and for a while Horatio and Hamlet watch and listen unobserved, in a "showing" scene of the sort we have seen earlier. Finally Hamlet enters the action for approximately the last fifty lines.

Some producers and critics have felt this scene to be an afterthought (Evans 13; T. J. B. Spencer 331) because the *next* scene seems to begin with the talk Hamlet promised Horatio in his letter, the plot is not advanced here, and a pronounced shift in mood is necessary to take Hamlet from the grief, surprise, and anger of the end of 5.1 to the calm of his first words in 5.2. Some, such as David Garrick and Maurice Evans (emboldened by Garrick's example), have even felt justified in omitting the scene entirely. At the other end of the scale, scholars such as Maynard Mack and Roland Mushat Frye consider the scene to be the key to Hamlet's development in the play. For them, the scene's movement and iconography dramatize in small Hamlet's confrontation with death and the change from his impatience and self-criticism in the middle of the play to his readiness in the last scene (Mack 522–23; Frye 205).

For a scene this length, 5.1 achieves a fearful concentration because nothing escapes the centripetal concern with death. The main action displays two men who will shortly kill each other, grappling over the body of a woman newly dead and being buried. The questions of the scene, stemming from the main subject of death, concern what happens to the dead and to those left behind after a death. Where will the dead be buried—in or out of sanctified ground—and with what rites? How long will they lie in the earth before they rot, and what uses may their dust come to? As for their souls, will they become ministering angels or lie howling? The quick must be concerned with death, too—practically, as grave-makers, or personally, as mourning brothers, lovers, or friends. Will they mourn stoically or violently? Will they avenge those for whom they mourn, and if so, will they do it basely or straightforwardly? Will the knowledge that all must die affect their conduct?

The Clowns

The clowns' discussion neatly breaks in half: for the first twenty-five lines they discuss Ophelia's "doubtful" death and conclude that her Christian burial is a privilege of rank. For the latter twenty-five lines or so, they discuss the occupation of the gravedigger. These topics anticipate later, more serious conversations by the other players. Laertes and the priest will also debate over Ophelia's rites and the priest will remark that "great command o'ersways the order" that suicides should not lie in sanctified ground. Hamlet and Horatio will also discuss the gravedigger's occupation.

The First Clown begins, in the scene's and the play's dominant mode, with a question: "Is she to be buried in Christian burial when she willfully seeks her own salvation?" (1–2). More than a third of the play's scenes begin with a question in the first speech, and each of the sections into which I have divided this scene begins with a question. As audience, we register the Clown's malapropism and infer the intended *dam-nation*, infer also that Ophelia must be meant, and do so with surprise. Only twenty lines ago Gertrude described Ophelia's death as an accident. While the clowns discuss the mad idea that one can commit suicide in self-defense, we have time to assess this new mystery. Now Gertrude's speech a few lines before looks as if it might have concealed something, and what we were inclined to think stylization looks more like invention. However alert we may be for clues to resolve the mystery of Ophelia's death, we are bound to be disappointed. As Nigel Alexander writes in *Poison, Play, and Duel*, Shakespeare provides "in a few short scenes, the evidence for both prosecution and defence" (182). Here the Second Clown says the coroner "finds it Christian burial" (4)—one of those items in *Hamlet* that looks like evidence until it is undercut by the next suggestion. In this case the Second Clown suggests, and later the priest confirms, that the Christian burial of Ophelia followed a "great command," presumably from Claudius.

Has the king suborned the coroner? We might do better to ask why the issue of Ophelia's possible suicide has been brought up at all, let alone rendered so "doubtful." The problem of Ophelia's death shows again the difficulty of assigning motives to acts, or even distinguishing acts from accidents. Then too, Ophelia's possible suicide reminds us of Hamlet's options in dealing with his own grief; Ophelia and her brother are still reflecting Hamlet's choices in this scene, even after Ophelia's death.

The conclusion of the Second Clown is that Ophelia's burial in sanctified ground is a consequence of her rank: "Will you ha' the truth on't? If this had not been a gentlewoman, she should have been buried out o' Christian burial" (21–23). The Second Clown is little more than the butt of the First Clown's jokes, and thus he has little chance to become a character of any weight. But here he speaks the only lines in the play that come near to criticism of the class structure. At various times throughout *Hamlet* there are hints of how the play's events strike different classes differently. Examples are Marcellus's speech in 1.1 about how the war-watch, "So nightly toils the subject of the land," the conversation between the Captain and Hamlet in 4.4 over those soldiers who will die because "a delicate and tender prince" wants a worthless piece of ground, and Hamlet's remarks about Osric in 5.2: "Let a beast be lord of beasts, and his crib shall stand at the king's mess. 'Tis a chough, but, as I say, spacious in the possession of dirt" (87–89). We shall look further into this question of class differences in Hamlet's conversation with the gravedigger. But whatever the Second Clown may make of his lines here, the gravedigger turns the topic to the ridiculous: "Why, there thou say'st. And the more pity that great folk should have count'nance in this world to drown or hang themselves more than their even-Christen" (24–26). The gravedigger then shifts the conversation to his own occupation. The grave-maker's work spans the whole of human history. Digging was Adam's profession, and the grave-maker's work lasts till doomsday. The fact that the houses he makes are being continually broken up and their present tenants ejected to make way for new ones does not get into the gravedigger's riddle. Self-awareness is the key to how this character is played: he can be complacent and pompous in his displays of wit before the Second Clown and, later, Hamlet, or he can be unaffected and assured in his native cleverness.

He has a talent for the paradoxical. His instances are the "permanent" dwelling from which he is even now throwing the bones of former residents, the suicide who acts in self-defense, and Adam who is no gentleman because he digs (according to the old poem, "When Adam digged and Eve span / Who was then the gentleman?"), but who *is* a gentleman because he bore arms, needing them to dig.

In thus shifting the conversation to his occupation the gravedigger also opens the theme of time, which haunts this scene as it does no other in the play. The gravedigger sets the larger ranges of time's measurement, from creation to doomsday, and, in his song, the space of a man's life from youth to age. Hamlet asks how long the First Clown has been a gravedigger and how long it takes a corpse to rot. Specific times are mentioned: thirty years, three-and-twenty years, eight or nine years, three years.

"Whose grave's this?"

Hamlet's opening question asks how the First Clown can sing at grave-making. Horatio's answer might be taken to apply to more than the gravedigger's experience: "Custom hath made it in him a property of easiness" (64). Horatio may say the line as referring purely to the gravedigger, or, with some feeling, as applying to Hamlet's situation. That is, he may speak kindly ("thank heaven you have reached some similar easiness"), wishfully ("would that you had achieved such easiness"), or warily ("are you about to relapse from what serenity you have achieved?"). In any case, the opening exchange concerns getting used to death, and the gravedigger obliges by singing an apt verse and throwing up a skull. The gravedigger's song, which had sounded merry enough at its opening, turns lugubrious:

> But age with his stealing steps
> Hath clawed me in his clutch,
> And hath shipped me intil the land,
> As if I had never been such.
>
> (67–70)

The gravedigger's adoption of a song persona who is already dead is only one of the paradoxical features defining his relation to the others in the scene. He digs a grave that is his and not his; he "lies" in it while the dead Ophelia and the soon-to-be-dead Hamlet and Laertes "lie out on't" (114–15). As wit pretender, he bandies words with the real wit, and wins. His presence in the grave is by custom, choice, and long profession. The others are there by extraordinary happenstance to bury one who died by accident, or if by choice, only by deranged choice. He takes the role of current jester; the real jester is long dead, now providing only a foul smell and a *memento mori*.

The skulls thrown up by the gravedigger are emblems as well as the actual physical remains of death. Roland Mushat Frye has recently traced the broad iconographic background of Hamlet's contemplation of the skulls in this scene. The tradition of visual representation of a young man regarding a skull was already a century and a half old on the continent and at

least half a century old in England by the time *Hamlet* was written (Frye 207–14). Shakespeare introduced it to drama, where
it was immediately used by other dramatists, most notably by
Tourneur in *The Revenger's Tragedy,* where the skull becomes
the play's main symbol. In *Hamlet* the protagonist's contemplation of the skull is not only the central image of this scene, but
the most important image of the play in the *memory's* eye.
Some productions have Hamlet seizing the first skull eagerly,
but the dialogue does not indicate that Hamlet handles any
skull before he asks to see Yorick's (172), and the text warrants
some revulsion: Kozintsev has his Hamlet gag at the skull, and
every Hamlet says "My gorge rises at it" (176) of Yorick's skull.
He may be both fascinated and repelled at the same time.

Hamlet's "applications" begin with a politician and a
courtier. According to Mack, he confronts death in "ever more
poignant" and specific terms, progressing from the anony-
mous courtiers and lawyers to Yorick, whom he knew, and finally to Ophelia, whom he loved (522). But the language
Hamlet uses at seeing the first skull thrown out by the gravedigger may allow us to conclude that he thinks immediately of
his father and Polonius:

> That skull had a tongue in it, and could sing once. How the
> knave jowls it to the ground, as if 'twere Cain's jawbone,
> that did the first murther! This might be the pate of a
> politician, which this ass now o'erreaches; one that would
> circumvent God, might it not? (71–75)

The only other mention of Cain in the play occurs in reference
to Hamlet's father, when Claudius says his crime has "the pri-
mal eldest curse upon't, / A brother's murder" (3.2.37–38). Polonius certainly aspired to be a politician, and Hamlet knows
two of the most recent additions to this graveyard are his father
and Polonius.

Hamlet's first set of applications has to do with power and
station: the politician who would circumvent God, the courtier
and the lord. The second set has to do with occupations of law
and land-buying. Hamlet compares the situation of the dead
with the exercise of power by the living, with the delights of
station and of occupation, of acquisition, of making small dis-

tinctions (quiddities, quillities, and tricks). The dead have suffered a revolution; equal and powerless, they are "my Lady Worm's" subjects, "Knocked about the mazzard with a sexton's spade," without influence, without property beyond the dirt in their skulls, evicted even from the grave to make room for another of their number.

This conversation, more like a monologue, stimulates Hamlet's curiosity to know who the grave's new tenant will be. He turns from the somewhat rarified quibbles he has been making with Horatio to shorter, broader exchanges with the grave-maker.

The encounter between the sexton and Hamlet can be pleasant enough; the two friends are patient and indulgent with a working man who pretends to wit and entertains them and himself while he works at a job most would consider unsavory. The spotlight stays on the prince. Another reading places more emphasis on the gravedigger's jokes, not as knee-slapping humor, but as a very well-played set of the game called *getting the best of the gentleman*. A fairly complex shift of sympathies can take place in this part of the scene, to the extent that we may not be seeing it at all from Hamlet's class viewpoint when we hear him say "By the Lord, Horatio, this three years I have taken note of it, the age is grown so picked that the toe of the peasant comes so near the heel of the courtier he galls his kibe" (129–32). In the wordplay, Hamlet is bested on *lie*—"You lie out on't sir" (115)—which may simply mean you are not in it, but may also give Hamlet the lie without committing the sexton; on *quick*; on *man* and *woman*; on *came to be mad* and *ground*. In the meantime, Hamlet has been called a fool or worse (137). Possibly the gravedigger's remark about "pocky corses" is a class criticism. Finally, it is at least likely that the gravedigger's figure for how long a body will lie in the earth before it rots is so outrageously long just to see if the gentleman will buy it—and he apparently does.

Hamlet is interested in graves. He has perhaps heard the old advice that before setting out on revenge one should first dig two graves. But he does not find out from the sexton whom this grave is for. He changes tack and asks how long the grave-maker has been at his occupation. The answer comes back in pieces: "I came to't that day our last king Hamlet overcame Fortinbras. . . . It was the very day that young Hamlet was born. . . . I have been sexton here, man and boy, thirty years" (134–35, 137–38, 151–52). The coincidence, not the first in the play, means that the motive of young Fortinbras's revenge is just as old as young Hamlet. It means that the story of his father's heroism has been with Hamlet since his birth, which helps to explain his hyperboles about his father at 1.2.139–53 and 3.4.56–64.

Hamlet's response to the gravedigger's remark that he has "been sexton here, man and boy, thirty years" is to ask "How long will a man lie i' th' earth ere he rot?" (153). Hamlet may be thinking of his own body, having taken to heart the contemporaneity and symbolic association of his life with the gravedigger's trade. On the other hand, he may just be looking for an expert opinion, now that he is on the ground and on the subject, from a man who has made it his work for so long. Or he may be thinking of his father. Could one of these skulls be old Hamlet? When scholars defend the discrepancy between Hamlet's youth at the beginning of the play and his obvious age of thirty here, they say it gives the effect of Hamlet's emotional growth and maturity. They do not mention that it also may suggest that old Hamlet has been in his grave quite a long time. But whether the time has been long or short, Hamlet does know, or ought to know, that a man rots before "eight or nine year," even in a cold country ("But if indeed you find him not within this month, you shall nose him as you go up the stairs into the lobby"—4.3.35–36).

"Here's a skull now hath lien you i' th' earth three-and-twenty years," says the gravedigger, and this second skull is very particularly identified. Where the first skull might have been a politician, a courtier, a lawyer, land-buyer, or possibly even old Hamlet himself, the identity of the second one is insistently discussed, so that the most inattentive spectator must notice it. When Hamlet asks whose it was, the gravedigger teases him: "Whose do you think it was?" Hamlet's "Nay, I know not" has the force of repeating his question, and this time the answer comes, but with a pause to further concentrate attention: "This same skull, sir, was—sir—Yorick's skull, the king's jester" (168–69). Still another exchange draws back the inattentive before Hamlet takes the skull and speaks his "Alas, poor Yorick" speech: "This? . . . E'en that . . . Let me see" (170–72).

Hamlet's lines about Yorick are not the best known in the play, but the tableau of the young man with the skull is the best known visual image of the play. The speech is a focus for all the play's themes on death; it begins with *ubi sunt* and ends with *respice finem*. If we may imagine Hamlet's contemplation of the skull to be another "showing," it is one in which the jester takes the part of death and vice-versa, though neither is assuming a role. Hamlet's old play companion is now his object lesson and moral messenger: "Now get you to my lady's chamber, and tell her, let her paint an inch thick, to this favor she must come" (180–82). It is usually assumed that Hamlet is referring to his mother, and the remark fits with much that Hamlet has said to her from the beginning of the play ("Ay, madam, it [death] is common" [1.2.74]) through the scene in her closet where he urged her to assume a virtue even if she did not have it. But we should remember that Hamlet does not yet know Ophelia is dead and could be referring to her as "my lady"; it is Ophelia after all whom Hamlet talked about before in connection with "painting" (3.1.142).

Horatio answers affirmatively when Hamlet asks whether the dead Alexander looked and smelled as Yorick does now, but when Hamlet imagines Alexander's dust stopping a bunghole, Horatio says that he is considering "too curiously" (193). Horatio may fear that Hamlet is skirting close to matters that are too disturbing when he begins to muse on the death and dissolution of kings. Or Horatio may merely lack the imagination to follow Alexander or Caesar plugging holes in a wall or a beer barrel. Hamlet has already suggested that his philosophy is too limited (1.5.166–67); if it is, this response may signal that Horatio knows it, even defends it in his way.

"What ceremony else?"

When Ophelia's funeral procession enters, Hamlet de-
duces the station and the suspected suicide of "the corse they
follow" from the incomplete ceremony and the presence of the
royal couple and courtiers. His instinct, out of delicacy, cunning, or fear, is to listen without being observed, and so he
does, with Horatio. He observes a "show" in which Laertes
argues with the priest, who becomes for the moment a kind of
surrogate revenge object, not having killed Laertes' sister, but
having denied her the burial service. Thus Hamlet sees how
Laertes deals with grief and the desire for vengeance. In the
process Hamlet acquires another source of grief himself, if we
admit the love he here claims for Ophelia.

Laertes' twice-repeated question "What ceremony else?"
brings the Doctor's response:

> Her death was doubtful,
> And, but that great command o'ersways the order,
> She should in ground unsanctified have lodged
> Till the last trumpet. For charitable prayers,
> Shards, flints, and pebbles should be thrown on her.
> Yet here she is allowed her virgin crants.
> Her maiden strewments, and the bringing home
> Of bell and burial.
>
> (214–21)

Our response to the dispute between Laertes and the Doctor
has more complexity than mere sympathy with the bereaved
brother. The Doctor can be seen as one of the king's toadies
who was influenced to bury Ophelia in sanctified ground but
who would not go farther to allow her the burial service;
against this figure we side with Laertes, and find the "shards,
flints, and pebbles" speech gratuitously cruel and "churlish."
On the other hand, the clowns have suspected that the rules
applying to all the rest of us have been lifted for this woman
because she is "great folk," and now Laertes is demanding
even more. The Doctor thus can become a conservative representative of the people against the corruption of power, while
Laertes and Claudius are now together on the other side from

our sympathies. This shift is made more possible because of Laertes' ambivalent position in our sympathies, even before he opens his mouth. His bereavement seems to demand our sympathy, but his conspiracy with the king pushes him to the side of villainy.

Laertes' expression of vengeful frustration is to tell the priest he will be in hell when Ophelia is a "minist'ring angel." The tension of this confrontation is then diffused by Gertrude's placing or strewing of flowers and the sad speech about her futile wish for Hamlet's and Ophelia's union. Gertrude's mention of Hamlet's name reminds Laertes of the real object of his revenge:

> O, treble woe
> Fall ten times treble on that cursèd head
> Whose wicked deed thy most ingenious sense
> Deprived thee of!
> (233–36)

His extravagant expression of grief is the wish to be buried alive with his sister:

> Now pile your dust upon the quick and dead
> Till of this flat a mountain you have made
> T' o'ertop old Pelion or the skyish head
> Of blue Olympus.
> (238–41)

Hazlitt's word for Laertes' language was *rhodomontade* (237). Here it provokes Hamlet from his hiding place.

". . . the present push"

Hamlet reenters the action with a question (few of his speeches in this scene are without a question): "What is he whose grief / Bears such an emphasis?" (241–42). At the same time he identifies himself: "This is I, Hamlet the Dane" (244–45). Laertes seizes him. Hamlet asks Laertes to take his fingers from his throat in a speech that sounds very controlled, but both king and queen speak of Hamlet's "fit" and his madness

here, and even Horatio begs Hamlet to calm himself. When
Horatio speaks to him, Hamlet answers that he will fight
Laertes on this theme until his eyelids "will no longer wag"
(254). The theme is grief and its expression. There is much variation possible in the relation between Hamlet's grief and
Laertes'. This Hamlet may be thoroughly in control and making a deliberate show of passion to berate Laertes for the whin-
ing, ranting, posturing way in which Laertes is dealing with
his grief, or Hamlet may have really lost control, either at his
own image reflected in Laertes' grief, or because of Ophelia's
death. Hamlet makes an unequivocal statement of his love for
Ophelia, quite different from the changeable way he spoke to
her of his love at 3.1.115 and 119–20.

After his outburst, Hamlet speaks more quietly to Laertes:

> Hear you, sir.
> What is the reason that you use me thus?
> I loved you ever. But it is no matter.
> Let Hercules himself do what he may,
> The cat will mew, and dog will have his day.
>
> (275–79)

Hamlet then exits, or allows himself to be led off by Horatio.

The king's speech to Laertes reminds him of their plot and
looks toward the play's last movement:

> Strengthen your patience in our last night's speech.
> We'll put the matter to the present push.—
> This grave shall have a living monument.
> An hour of quiet shortly shall we see;
> Till then in patience our proceeding be.
>
> (281–85)

Though Claudius mentions patience twice in this speech, he is
counseling immediate action. The pace of this scene has accel-
erated from calm to passion (as the next scene will do to an
even greater degree) while the play moves toward its climax.
The compression in the time imagery reflects the acceleration:
where we began with the whole span of the created world and
the time from man's youth to his age, we have now arrived at
an ironic "hour of quiet" and "the present push."

Scene Two

The previous scene is perhaps the only "showing" scene in which the spectators (Hamlet, Horatio, and the audience) get full and correct information about what is going on. It begins as hidden espials but moves to a disclosure of the spectators to the participants, a disclosure that leads to violence as in 3.4, although the disclosure is voluntary in 5.1. The duel in the last scene of the play is also the last "showing" scene, one that begins with two participants, Hamlet and Laertes, and gradually opens to involve each of the onstage spectators in the action. At the end, Fortinbras, though he comes asking, "Where is this sight," acts rather than looks on at another show: he salutes Hamlet's death and prepares to become Horatio's audience, replacing us as Hamlet's story is told again. As for us, we are included in the direction *Exeunt*. We exit, not the stage but the theater or the book, with Hamlet's story in our mind's eye.

At almost four hundred lines, 5.2 is the second longest scene in the play, with much humor, action, and relation of past events. It is like the previous scene in deriving unity from concentration on death, but where the previous scene looked at death from after the fact (those newly dead or long dead), this scene looks at approaching death, hastened by plots. At the beginning, Hamlet tells of a plot intended to kill him, turned around into a plot to kill Rosencrantz and Guildenstern. Osric enters to entice Hamlet into Laertes' plot to kill the prince. Hamlet and Laertes duel, Hamlet is killed in accordance with the plot, but Hamlet turns it around and kills Laertes with it as well. Meanwhile Gertrude is killed by the poison, Claudius's back-up plot to kill Hamlet. Hamlet, discovering all, uses Laertes' and Claudius's plot instruments, envenomed sword and poison cup, to kill Claudius. Hamlet must restrain Horatio from killing himself by means of the poison. After Hamlet's death, the ambassadors enter to tell of the success of the plot Hamlet described at the scene's beginning.

Horatio says he will explain all these plots and tell

> Of carnal, bloody, and unnatural acts,
> Of accidental judgments, casual slaughters,
> Of deaths put on by cunning and forced cause,
> And, in this upshot, purposes mistook
> Fall'n on th' inventors' heads.
>
> (370–74)

The catalogue may even include the possible self-destruction of Ophelia and Horatio's own averted self-destruction, as well as the belated vengeful killing of Claudius.

"So Rosencrantz and Guildenstern go to't"

Hamlet has been talking, and as in 5.1, the talk is not so much a conversation between Horatio and Hamlet as it is Hamlet's forum, where he now explains not only the circumstances of his replacement of Rosencrantz and Guildenstern's commission with one he composes, but also his attitudes—toward impulsive action, toward the deaths of Rosencrantz and Guildenstern, toward the king, toward the short time he has left, and toward Laertes.

Hamlet praises rashness in a typically problematic speech:

> Rashly,
> And praised be rashness for it—let us know,
> Our indiscretion sometimes serves us well
> When our deep plots do pall, and that should learn us
> There's a divinity that shapes our ends,
> Rough-hew them how we will—
>
> (6–11)

Although there is no textual problem in the speech there are questions it raises, and not merely minor ones such as that of its syntactical connections—not clear until Hamlet's next speech. It is a well-known speech, often misquoted (as *teach* for *learn*), and seemingly contradicted by at least one other of Hamlet's speeches: "I am not splenitive and rash" (5.1.248).

Moreover it is morally problematic, putting piety to work in justification of an arguably gratuitous killing.

There is some convergence of possible readings as the play nears its end: how many possibilities can be imagined for "O villainy! Ho! let the door be locked. Treachery! Seek it out"? (300–301). But the most puzzling questions about character and morality remain. For example, one view of Hamlet is as a clearly heroic rather than villainous revenger. He does not plot or hasten his revenge of Claudius. But his last scene begins with a description of how he sent Rosencrantz and Guildenstern to their deaths. He seems to take pleasure in the mechanism of their disposal—at least he wants to describe it to Horatio: "Wilt thou know / Th' effect of what I wrote?" (36–37). He arrives at the plan in an almost automatic or unconscious way:

> Being thus benetted round with villainies,
> Or I could make a prologue to my brains,
> They had begun the play. I sat me down,
> Devised a new commission.
>
> (29–32)

Even Horatio may have trouble stomaching his friend's action. "So Rosencrantz and Guildenstern go to't" (56), he says, and after Hamlet's speech about their making love to their employment (in the Folio only) and their deaths not being near his conscience, Horatio's response is to shift attention: "Why, what a king is this!" (63). Every Horatio can condemn Claudius, though some may stick at acquitting Hamlet. In the BBC version Robert Swann looked at the floor while Hamlet justified his disposal of Rosencrantz and Guildenstern, then looked up for "what a king is this." Even the tone is not surely read from the text in much of the scene. The very quiet delivery of the scene's first lines, for example, may be a modern "tradition" going back no farther than Booth (Shattuck 268).

The replacement of the commission is one of those many scenes that the theater audience must create in the mind's eye as the reader creates all of *Hamlet*. Not accidentally, these "unplayed" scenes keep dark the answers to the play's main questions. We need not go back so far as the question whether

Gertrude was an adulteress and an accessory to her husband's murder. Was Hamlet mad or merely shamming when he approached Ophelia in her closet? Does Hamlet board the pirate ship out of courage or out of desperation? Does he gleefully send Rosencrantz and Guildenstern to their deaths, or can he not defend himself otherwise from what they may say of Claudius's purposes?

Having shown Horatio Claudius's commission ordering his execution, Hamlet asks about his justification in killing the king:

> Does it not, think thee, stand me now upon—
> He that hath killed my king, and whored my mother,
> Popped in between th' election and my hopes,
> Thrown out his angle for my proper life,
> And with such coz'nage—is't not perfect conscience
> To quit him with this arm? And is't not to be damned
> To let this canker of our nature come
> In further evil?
>
> (63–70)

This is the closest Hamlet ever gets to questioning whether his purpose in revenging his father is subject to conscience. Horatio's answer could hardly be more equivocal.

> It must be shortly known to him from England
> What is the issue of the business there.
>
> (71–72)

Does Horatio mean "*yes* and you had better do it because you have little time," or is he avoiding the question by reminding Hamlet of his danger, or is he merely not wasting words on a question that needs no answer, either because Hamlet will accept only one answer or because the answer is obviously yes?

Hamlet agrees that the time will be short, but also says that the interim is his. He also voices his sorrow at forgetting himself to Laertes.

> For by the image of my cause I see
> The portraiture of his. I'll court his favors.
>
> (77–78)

Thus we are prepared for Hamlet's apology to Laertes before it is requested by Gertrude.

"The king, sir, hath wagered with him"

A sizable chunk of the final scene, more than a hundred lines, is given to exchanges with "young Osric." The modern stage tradition plays Osric as foppish, with usually a suggestion of homosexuality, although much of the dialogue suggests he is merely very affected, with French manners, and very young: he is twice called "young Osric," and the pair of lines about the lapwing running away with the shell on its head and Osric complying with his dug before he sucked it seems to stress the point. The foppishness certainly works, and in support of it, the First Quarto has a direction reading "*Enter a Bragart Gentleman*" at Osric's entrance. But the idea of a very young heir who fancies himself the complete courtier works also and creates contrasts among the maturity of Hamlet and Horatio, the immaturity of Laertes, and the comic extremity of immaturity, pretending to something more, in Osric. In the space devoted to comic matters in both of the last two scenes of the play, as we move into more sorrow and deaths, there is evidence for De Quincey's observation, in "On the Knocking at the Gate in *Macbeth*" (1823), that "action in any direction is best expounded, measured, and made apprehensible, by reaction" (1094).

Osric advances the plot in summoning Hamlet to the contest set up by the king and Laertes; he is also a conspirator himself, as may be seen at 295; but he is first a clown who engages unwillingly and apparently unknowingly in wit-combat with Hamlet. His function and that of the gravedigger in 5.1 are thus parallel, but the characters are antithetical: the gravedigger is innocent, plain, of mature years and lower class; he gets the best of his verbal bouts with Hamlet. Osric is an accomplice, fancy in his language and, by stage tradition, his dress; he is young and, if not titled, at least rich, "spacious in the possession of dirt"; and he is bested by Hamlet and Horatio without ever quite knowing what is happening.

Osric's errand is to place before Hamlet the terms of the duel. Claudius has made it attractive by the odds on Hamlet's side; the king may also have the shrewdness to see the appeal, to one of Hamlet's temperament, in the prospect of apologizing graciously to Laertes and then besting him at the very sport in which he is reputed to excel. Osric cannot suspect that Hamlet might say no.

> OSRIC. The king, sir, hath laid, sir, that in a dozen passes between yourself and him he shall not exceed you three hits; he hath laid on twelve for nine, and it would come to immediate trial if your lordship would vouchsafe the answer.
> HAMLET. How if I answer no?
> OSRIC. I mean, my lord, the opposition of your person in trial.
>
> (159–66)

But Hamlet, after this moment of suspense, accepts the challenge.

"I shall win at the odds"

Hamlet, in answer to Horatio's comment that Laertes will win, says "I do not think so" and goes on to say that he has been in "continual practice" since Laertes went to France. This does not accord with his saying to Rosencrantz and Guildenstern that he has "forgone all custom of exercises" (2.2.293), but it seems to be borne out later when he quickly wins the first two hits of the duel. Although his doubts are not about winning, but more vague, he will not let Horatio stop the duel. Earlier, he had said that, though the time until Claudius discovered the fate of Rosencrantz and Guildenstern would be short, it was *his* time, and "a man's life no more than to say 'one' " (74). Now he defies "augury":

> There is special providence in the fall of a sparrow. If it be now, 'tis not to come; if it be not to come, it will be now; if it be not now, yet it will come. The readiness is all. Since no man of aught he leaves knows, what is't to leave betimes? Let be. (208–13)

Is this patience or fatalism? Is Hamlet courageous in defying what fears he has, "such a kind of gaingiving as would perhaps trouble a woman" (205)? Is he foolhardy in failing to remember that the fears that troubled Andromache or Caesar's wife were not hysteria? Johnson was able to find in Hamlet's words a laudable scorn for "the superstition of augury and omens, which has no ground in reason or piety" (194). For Coleridge the passage was evidence of Shakespeare's "fondness for presentiment" (1:36–37). Whether Shakespeare was fond of such omens or not, some would say he manages to have both superstition and piety, including the omens and having Hamlet scorn them.

The royal party enters, and the duel goes forward.

"A hit, a very palpable hit"

But first Hamlet makes a lengthy apology to Laertes. Johnson did not approve of the speech: "it is unsuitable to the character of a good or a brave man, to shelter himself in falsehood" (195). And it would be difficult to prove that Hamlet believes the truth of all he says in this speech. Perhaps it would be easier to argue that Hamlet is neither good nor brave, and that this falsehood is far from his first in the play. The counter-argument is that he has told Horatio that he is "very sorry" that he "forgot" himself to Laertes, and this apology is hardly more than a conventional statement of his regret, the "gentle entertainment" his mother has called for and Hamlet has approved (195–97). And the irony of the latter view is that Hamlet speaks false while intending a true apology, while Laertes speaks false in accepting it and saying he "will not wrong" Hamlet's offered love, when he is about to murder him.

The duel itself can be staged dozens of different ways. In winning the first touches Hamlet may, in fact, be the better swordsman, or he may be lucky, or he may be correct in thinking Laertes is merely dallying with him. Laertes has reason to be nervous, and possibly the conscience he speaks of at 285

restrains him from playing as well as he can. Laertes strikes
Maurice Evans's Hamlet in the back at "Have at you now,"
when a bout is supposed to have been terminated by Osric's
"Nothing neither way" (Evans 182). Many productions approach the wounding more squeamishly, having Laertes
merely pierce Hamlet's wrist (Olivier) or arm (BBC). None of
the texts indicates that the wounds need be slight, however.
We should not forget that the scheme plotted by Laertes and
the king calls for Hamlet to be killed by the unbated sword,
and the poison is merely an addition for security's sake. Of
course a slight wound may be a way of dramatizing Laertes'
pang of conscience (285), yet he knows the poison will work in
only a scratch.

While the main contest goes on at the center of attention,
Claudius prepares his "back or second" to the plot, and sees it
miss its mark, killing the queen. He places the poison, in the
guise of "an union" (the word sets up Hamlet's last quibble), in
the cup after Hamlet wins the first hit (271). Hamlet refuses
Claudius's urging to drink (273), but after the second hit,
Gertrude takes the cup: "The queen carouses to thy fortune,
Hamlet" (278). The moment is charged with irony and Gertrude's gesture capable of being played a number of ways:

> Gertrude is showing something of her appetites. The ex-
> citement of the duel stimulates them, and she drinks even
> in defiance of Claudius's request, order, or warning:
> "Gertrude, do not drink." This reading fits with a general
> characterization of Gertrude as a creature of appetite; the
> irony here is that she, as the appetitive object which is the
> cause of all the conflicts in the play, is the first casualty
> because of appetite.

> Gertrude's is a maternal gesture: getting the child to accept
> the offered food or drink by taking some of it first. Since
> the cup is Claudius's offering, the gesture urges Hamlet's
> acceptance of Claudius and recalls similar implicit pleas
> in 1.2.

Gertrude is allying herself with Claudius by taking the cup, even though he tells her not to drink. She is imitating the king's gesture: "The king shall drink to Hamlet's better breath . . . 'Now the king drinks to Hamlet' " (260, 267). She is clearly signalling to Hamlet that she is not following the instructions he gives her in the closet scene. The irony here is that Claudius's plot kills her even as she attempts to move closer to him by this act.

Gertrude knows the cup is poisoned, or very strongly suspects it, and she drinks to save Hamlet. She is most literally drinking to his fortune, but deliberately turning her own ill. This is Olivier's interpretation, in which Eileen Herlie sees what is afoot as soon as Basil Sydney drops his pearl ring into the cup. She looks at the cup while the second bout is being played, considering what she will do. Then she takes it and immediately drinks. Olivier moves lines slightly, but need not; the text will support this interpretation, which is to some extent bolstered by the queen's later certainty that the drink has poisoned her (299).

Why does Claudius fail to stop Gertrude from drinking the poison? He may be physically unable to do so because courtiers intervene until it is too late. Guthrie staged the scene in this way, with a "traffic jam" at the moment the king wishes to get to Gertrude (Rossi 59). In Olivier's version, Claudius cannot stop the queen because she moves to drink the poison too quickly and purposefully. In both these cases, Claudius is prevented from shouting to Gertrude by the fear of his plan being revealed, just as in other readings he is rendered immovable by the same fear. In still others, he seems to be immobilized inexplicably, as if he realized her act was retribution and could not be stopped even if he tried.

After the change of rapiers (only the Folio has the direction, but Laertes' words at 295 make it clear what has happened), the action moves very fast. The queen dies, after saying that the drink is poisoned (299). Laertes confesses his own treachery with the "unbated and envenomed" sword (306) and the king's treachery with the poison (308). Hamlet stabs Claudius (311) and forces him to drink the poison as well:

> Here, thou incestuous, murd'rous, damnèd Dane,
> Drink off this potion. Is thy union here?
> Follow my mother.
>
> (314–16)

Hamlet puns on Claudius's union with Gertrude in death. It is the last of the marriages of love and death in the play's imagery.

". . . report me and my cause aright"

Hamlet exchanges forgiveness with Laertes, who dies at 320. Only two concerns remain: publishing the truth of what has just taken place, and settling the succession to the throne of Denmark. Hamlet himself would be the ideal reporter of his story, but he cannot, as he tells those onstage and the rest of us:

> You that look pale and tremble at this chance,
> That are but mutes or audience to this act,
> Had I but time—as this fell sergeant, Death,
> Is strict in his arrest—O, I could tell you—
> But let it be. Horatio, I am dead;
> Thou livest; report me and my cause aright
> To the unsatisfied.
>
> (323–29)

When Horatio starts to drink the poison, Hamlet prevents him, and continues his request that Horatio report his cause:

> O God, Horatio, what a wounded name,
> Things standing thus unknown, shall live behind me!
> If thou didst ever hold me in thy heart,
> Absent thee from felicity awhile,
> And in this harsh world draw thy breath in pain,
> To tell my story.
>
> (333–38)

There is some evidence in these two speeches to support those (for example, Werder 43–54) who argue that Hamlet's delay has been caused by the necessity for public indictment of Claudius rather than for his death alone. The "mutes or audience to this act" who are *onstage* do not know the circumstances leading up to "this act" as we do, and thus are "unsatisfied." Hamlet has a "wounded name" because he bears the reputation of madness and the accusation of treason that was the courtiers' reaction to his stabbing of Claudius at 312. On the other hand, it is only reasonable that Hamlet should wish the truth known, and the misapprehension of those present has not prevented him from killing Claudius.

Hamlet's last breath is spent in giving his voice for Fortinbras's succession, as well as stating his wish that the Norwegian prince be told what led up to the present slaughter.

"Go, bid the soldiers shoot"

With the entrance of Fortinbras with ambassadors from England, the outside world does more than merely touch or visit the closed, claustrophobic society of Elsinore; it opens up the dark places to the light. Fortinbras enters at 351 with a question: "Where is this sight?" None of the editions I have looked at comments on this, but it is curious. If Fortinbras has just been warned what to expect, who has left the scene to do it?

A studied parallelism links this scene with the first court scene (1.2). Ambassadors from England arrive here with news that orders the king never gave have been performed. In 1.2, ambassadors to Norway were dispatched with careful instructions and "delated articles." In 1.2, a new king assumed his throne "with wisest sorrow" for the death of the previous one. Here Fortinbras assumes the throne by saying "with sorrow I embrace my fortune" (377). In both scenes Claudius makes a point of the cannon announcing his toasts to heaven and heaven echoing them back to earth, but here the king's last "carouse" is forced and poisoned, and the last cannon salutes Hamlet.

The very end, like the very first scene, is solemn and martial. Fortinbras's last speech uses the word *soldier* repeatedly: "Bear Hamlet like a soldier . . . and for his passage / The soldiers' music. . . . / Go, bid the soldiers shoot."

Fortinbras takes over quietly enough. To some extent he is merely doing what he is told; Horatio tells him what to do (366–69) and then suggests he do it quickly (382–84). But there is no doubt that the third revenger has come into his own. Hamlet, Laertes, and Fortinbras all threatened to take over the throne in one way or another during the play. Hamlet was "the most immediate" to it and literally held a sword over Claudius in the middle and at the end of the play. Laertes was at least momentarily the people's choice at one point. Fortinbras, who claims "some rights of memory in this kingdom," has been a threat in the background since the beginning, and now has a battle-ready army behind him, as well as Hamlet's dying voice for the succession. A kind of order will be restored, though Hamlet's ambiguous description of Fortinbras as "a delicate and tender prince" leaves possible an ending that has more of doubt than calm hope.

The only thing left undone as the stage empties is Horatio's account "to th' yet unknowing world / How these things came about" (368–69). Horatio has most carefully and solemnly been charged with two tasks during the play. The first is to be a witness. At the beginning of the play, he attests to the ghost's reality. Later, he watches Claudius's behavior at the play within the play. Throughout, he observes the course of Hamlet's story, even as we do. His second task is to be a reporter of these things he has witnessed. Horatio is to tell Hamlet's story, the most solemn charge, repeated three times in Hamlet's dying words (328, 338, 346). Hamlet lives on in Horatio for as long as the fiction lasts. In the fiction, as we might extend it, Horatio tells Hamlet's story, which becomes legend, is reported, is made a play and performed for audiences like us. But in effect it is we, the audience, identified with Horatio all along, who are to carry his story with us to the world outside the play. Hamlet becomes his audience completely at the end of the play. After the soldiers shoot, Hamlet is again only in our mind's eye.

Epilogue
Watching Ourselves:
What Happens (To the Reader)
in Hamlet

The theatrical self-reference of *Hamlet* is intimately con-
nected to its tentativeness and multivalence. Hamlet begins by
arguing for genuineness of feeling against the false representation of performance, in his first speech of any length:

> Seems, madam? Nay, it is. I know not 'seems.'
> 'Tis not alone my inky cloak, good mother,
> Nor customary suits of solemn black,
> Nor windy suspiration of forced breath,
> No, nor the fruitful river in the eye,
> Nor the dejected havior of the visage,
> Together with all forms, moods, shapes of grief,
> That can denote me truly. These indeed seem,
> For they are actions that a man might play,
> But I have that within which passeth show—
> These but the trappings and the suits of woe.
>
> (1.2.76–86)

Soliloquizing at the end of this scene, he admits that he *is* acting, at least in restraint, by holding his tongue (159). When the
ghost has delivered its message, Hamlet talks about the possible need to put an antic disposition on (1.5.172), a kind of role
playing he will later call being "idle" (3.2.87). Hamlet starts an
impromptu reading of a piece of *Dido and Aeneas;* he writes for,
stage manages, and prompts a production of *The Murder of
Gonzago;* and he prepares himself by working up mood and
action for a scene with his mother. He plays a ranting part—"a
part to tear a cat in," as Bottom says of heroic roles in *A Mid-
summer Night's Dream*—when he wants to show Laertes to himself in the graveyard (5.1.241ff.), but shortly before his death he

apologizes to Laertes by saying that the Hamlet who insulted or wronged him was merely a character played involuntarily (5.2.215–33). Some roles Hamlet will not play. Francis Barker sees the whole course of action in *Hamlet* as a series of refusals to play certain parts: "the roles of courtier, lover, son, politician, swordsman, and so on" (35). But Hamlet engages with other roles, for shorter or longer periods, sometimes tentatively and sometimes with great gusto and conviction. Some of these roles are incompatible with others: Hamlet's part actively contradicts its own interpretations, while those of Claudius and Gertrude, for example, merely omit information that would settle some of the many questions about how their parts are to be read. The pace and rhythm of each scene in *Hamlet* are those of a whole performance, but the mood and atmosphere surrounding the protagonist are those of a rehearsal. Gielgud seized on this aspect of the play when staging his 1963–64 "rehearsal" *Hamlet* with Richard Burton in the lead; this quality of the play is also what gives it its familiar resemblance to the sometimes dreadful improvisations of real life. *Hamlet* resembles life in that its improvisations are just as frightening as its inevitabilities. The way the play reflects life, and vice-versa, is dizzying, like regressive mirror images. Hamlet frequently seems to be rehearsing for a possible play while the rest of the ensemble are acting in quite another, real one. The easiest way for them to deal with this lack of synchrony is to call it madness. If madness is an unwillingness to choose one arbitrary reality and exclude the rest, then Hamlet is indeed thoroughly mad, but it is the madness of his audience as well. Hazlitt said "It is *we* who are Hamlet" (232). The prince may be forgiven some indecision in having to take on all of our indecisions.

One consequence of the fact that we are Hamlet is that all of the critical problems of the play become our problems. What have traditionally been seen as problems of the play or of the protagonist become the reader's problems. Is Hamlet mad? For the reader, the issue of Hamlet's madness is no academic question, but an immediate one that must be decided again and again as the play is produced in the mind's eye. No scholarly argument or elaborate justification of absolute convictions is useful here; the play is waiting to go on. How can Hamlet's madness be played? This is the question the scholarly problem translates to. How will Hamlet read this speech if he is mad? How will his mother react when he reads it thus? Why will Claudius refuse to accept Hamlet's madness as real? What ironies are possible when Claudius, refusing to see Hamlet's real madness as other than madness in craft, yet says "Alas, alas" (4.3.26) to his speeches, implying to those assembled that Hamlet *is* really mad?

It is a saving fact, though, that what looks at first like the kaleidoscope of the play tends to organize itself into something more nearly like a spectrum when it is examined more closely. The varying interpretations of *Hamlet* turn out to have a limited range in their variations, a range that frequently simplifies further into a polar opposition between strength and weakness, complicity and innocence, or irony and single vision.

Concentrating on what is changeable about the text of *Hamlet*, as we have been doing for the last five chapters, has the effect of making what is unchangeable jump out in relief. What remains immutable, in every reading and production, among all the variations in the way characters speak to one another and react to each others' speeches, is a repeated, basic structure in scene after scene. *Hamlet* has a rhythm whose predictability works in counterpoint to the exploding possibilities of its every speech. The rhythm is that of the theatrical experience itself, of the play *in performance:* it is the rising and falling pattern of action taken from the time the theater is empty before the performance until it is empty once again at its end. Every Shakespearean scene begins and ends with a bare stage, but in *Hamlet*, individual scenes reproduce the same show and spectacle combined with mute observing that make up this particular play's shape. We watch the audience (Bernardo, Horatio and Marcellus) assemble for a frightening appearance; we wait while Bernardo recounts how this "dreaded sight [was] twice seen of us"; then we become the audience for the dreaded sight itself, twice in the first scene; finally we wonder mutely about its meaning as the onstage audience wonders aloud. The first scene shows us a pattern repeated in subsequent scenes: the whole performance is abstracted in the rhythm of the individual scene.

What happens to the reader as a result of this repetitive pattern? There is a certain steadying influence in the recurring rise and fall of the rhythm of each scene and thus something predictable running through the variety that Johnson called the play's distinguishing characteristic. But the main effect of the peculiar repetition of "showing" scenes is that it trains and prepares the reader for the play's main actions. Through the constant appearances and reappearances (the ghost's double appearance occurs both at the beginning and the end of Act One, for example) onstage spectators begin to assume the same importance as the matter they watch and hear: Horatio when the ghost speaks, Hamlet while Claudius recounts the recent court history of Denmark, Laertes and Ophelia while Polonius recites his "few precepts," Rosencrantz and Guildenstern while Hamlet tells them he has lost his pleasure in the world. During these scenes our gradual recognition that both spectacle and spectator deserve equal attention prepares us for the play's main acts, those which Nigel Alexander isolated as *poison, play,* and *duel.* We never see the first of these acts, the poisoning of old Hamlet, but we play it in the mind's eye as the ghost tells it, watch two recreations "something like" it at the dumb show and play within the play, and finally see mistaken, ironic, violent, and vengeful transformations of it in the poisonings of Gertrude and Claudius at the play's end. The play within the play, like each of the three acts of poison, play, and duel, contains the others, depicting the poisoning and being itself a duel of wit and conscience between Hamlet and Claudius. Hamlet instructs us even as he instructs Horatio how to watch, not the play, but the chief spectator. All the spectators interest us, including Hamlet, including ourselves. In the final scene of *Hamlet,* the spectators are either drawn in to death (Gertrude, Claudius) or to take a hand in the future telling of Hamlet's history. We become one with the onstage audience in this: Horatio will explain events to Fortinbras; we will

explain them to ourselves and others who are not yet *Hamlet's*
audience.

I have tried to show in some detail in the previous five
chapters what happens to one reader in *Hamlet*. If my own
experience is capable of extrapolation, other readers must be
also singularly challenged—challenged and torn by *Hamlet*.
Readers are tested by all drama, but *Hamlet* is a unique test.
The reader is torn between the desire to create a unified and
coherent Hamlet out of materials that want to fly apart, and the
desire to see how many Hamlets there really are—and readers
must find the limits of their imaginations. One part of the challenge is in attempting to find a single answer to the question,
What is going on? The other part of the challenge is in finding
how many answers there are to the same question. Each mind
is tested by *Hamlet* in that regard: is there another way, or another dozen ways, in which this speech can be read? Jack
Jorgens has written that the stage history of *Hamlet* attests to
the multivalence of all the principal roles: "We find records of
Polonius the likeable, well-meaning old man, and Polonius the
sly, knowing politician hiding behind a mask; Ophelia a sweet,
innocent girl, and Ophelia a spineless betrayer of the Prince;
Claudius the hedonistic slime of the earth, and Claudius the
capable ruler, sincere lover of Gertrude, and conscience-
stricken murderer" (208). The reader's experience reproduces
the stage history of *Hamlet*.

In our own persons and in those of our surrogates onstage,
we are bid throughout *Hamlet* to observe, listen, and judge.

> Well, sit we down,
> And let us hear Bernardo speak of this.
> (1.1.33–34)

> Observe my uncle . . . Give him heedful note.
> (3.2.77,81)

> And you, the judges, bear a wary eye.
> (5.2.268)

> You that look pale and tremble at this chance
> That are mutes or audience to this act. . . .
> (5.2.323–24)

But in Hamlet's person we do more than hear the tale; we play it again and again. As we play it, we change our minds about what it means. What happens in *Hamlet* is that the play trains us to take its parts of protagonist and audience both. The training is rigorous, and it never ends.

Works Cited

Alexander, Nigel. *Poison, Play, and Duel: A Study in Hamlet*. London: Routledge and Kegan Paul, 1971.

Barker, Francis. *The Tremulous Private Body: Essays on Subjection*. London: Methuen, 1984.

Benedix, Roderich. *Die Shakespearomanie*. Stuttgart: J. G. Cotta, 1873.

Booth, Stephen. "On the Value of *Hamlet*." In *Reinterpretations of Elizabethan Drama*, edited by Norman Rabkin, 137–76. New York: Columbia University Press, 1969.

Bowers, Fredson T. "Hamlet's Fifth Soliloquy, 3.2.406–17." In *Essays on Shakespeare and Elizabethan Drama in Honor of Hardin Craig*, edited by Richard Hosley, 213–22. Columbia: University of Missouri Press, 1962.

Bradley, A. C. *Shakespearean Tragedy*. 1904. Reprint. New York: Fawcett, 1965.

Bullough, Geoffrey, ed. *Narrative and Dramatic Sources of Shakespeare*. Vol. 7. London: Routledge and Kegan Paul, 1973.

Campbell, Lily Bess. *Shakespeare's Tragic Heroes: Slaves of Passion*. 1930. New York: Barnes and Noble, 1963.

Campbell, Oscar James, and Edward G. Quinn. *The Reader's Encyclopedia of Shakespeare*. New York: Thomas Y. Crowell, 1966.

Cassal, Gould. "Second String." *Brooklyn Daily Eagle* 18 October 1936: Section C. Reprinted in *Hamlet: Enter Critic*, edited by Claire Sacks and Edgar Whan, 33–34. New York: Appleton-Century-Crofts, 1960.

Champion, Larry. *Shakespeare's Tragic Perspectives*. Athens: University of Georgia Press, 1976.

Charney, Maurice. *Style in Hamlet*. Princeton: Princeton University Press, 1969.

Coleridge, Samuel Taylor. *Coleridge's Shakespearean Criticism*. Edited by Thomas M. Raysor. Cambridge: Harvard University Press, 1930.

De Quincey, Thomas. *Selected Writings of Thomas De Quincey*. Edited by Philip Van Doren Stern. New York: Random House, 1937.

Eliot, T. S. "Hamlet and His Problems." In *The Sacred Wood: Essays on Poetry and Criticism.* 1920. New York: Barnes and Noble, 1960. 95–103.

Empson, William. *The Structure of Complex Words.* New York: New Directions, 1951.

Evans, Maurice. *Maurice Evans' G. I. Production of "Hamlet."* Garden City, N.Y.: Doubleday, 1946.

Frye, Roland Mushat. *The Renaissance Hamlet.* Princeton: Princeton University Press, 1984.

Furness, Horace Howard, ed. *A New Variorum Edition of Shakespeare.* Vols. 3–4: *Hamlet.* Philadelphia: Lippincott, 1877. The reference is to volume 3 unless otherwise specified.

Gilbert, William S. *Rosencrantz and Guildenstern: A Tragic Episode, in Three Tableaux, Founded on an old Danish Legend.* In *Original Plays.* Third Series. London: Chatto & Windus, 1910.

Gilder, Rosamond. *John Gielgud's Hamlet: A Record of Performance.* London: Methuen, 1937.

Goethe, Johann Wolfgang von. *Wilhelm Meister's Apprenticeship.* Translated by Thomas Carlyle. Vol. 1. London: Chapman and Hall, 1870.

Gottschalk, Paul. *The Meanings of Hamlet: Modes of Literary Interpretation Since Bradley.* Albuquerque: University of New Mexico Press, 1972.

Granville-Barker, Harley. *Prefaces to Shakespeare. Third Series: Hamlet.* London: Sidgwick and Jackson, 1937.

Greenspun, Roger. Review of Tony Richardson's *Hamlet. New York Times* 22 December 1969: 43.

Hapgood, Robert. "Shakespeare and the Included Spectator." In *Reinterpretations of Elizabethan Drama,* 117–36. *See* Booth.

Harbage, Alfred. *As They Liked It: A Study of Shakespeare's Moral Artistry.* 1947. New York: Harper, 1961.

Harrison, G. B. *Shakespeare's Tragedies.* New York: Oxford University Press, 1951.

Hazlitt, William. *Characters of Shakespeare's Plays.* 1817. In *The Complete Works of William Hazlitt,* Edited by P. P. Howe, vol. 4. 1930. Reprint. New York: AMS Press, 1967.

Hedrick, Donald K. " 'It Is No Novelty for a Prince to be a Prince': An Enantiomorphous Hamlet." *Shakespeare Quarterly* 35(1984): 62–76.

Hunter, Robert G. *Shakespeare and the Mystery of God's Judgments.* Athens: University of Georgia Press, 1976.

Johnson, Samuel. *Johnson on Shakespeare: Essays and Notes Selected and Set Forth with an Introduction by Walter Raleigh.* London: Oxford University Press, 1908.

Jones, Ernest. *Hamlet and Oedipus.* New York: W. W. Norton, 1949.

Jorgens, Jack J. *Shakespeare on Film.* Bloomington: Indiana University Press, 1977.

Knight, G. Wilson. *The Imperial Theme.* 3d ed. London: Methuen, 1951.

———. *The Wheel of Fire.* London: Oxford University Press, 1930.

Knights, L. C. *Explorations: Essays in Criticism Mainly on the Literature of the Seventeenth Century.* New York: George W. Stewart, 1947.

Lamb, Charles. "On the Tragedies of Shakespeare, Considered with Reference to their Fitness for Stage Representation." (1811). In *The Works of Charles and Mary Lamb,* edited by E. V. Lucas, vol. 1:97–111. 1903. Reprint. New York: AMS Press, 1968.

Lavater, Lewes. *Of Ghostes and Spirites Walking by Nyght.* 1572. Edited by J. Dover Wilson and May Yardley. Oxford: Oxford University Press, 1929.

Leech, Clifford, "Studies in *Hamlet:* 1901–1955." *Shakespeare Survey* 9 (1956): 1–15.

Lewis, C. S. "Hamlet: The Prince or the Poem?" British Academy Annual Shakespeare Lecture, 1942. *Proceedings of the British Academy* 38. London: Oxford University Press, 1942.

Mack, Maynard. "The World of Hamlet." *The Yale Review* 41(1952): 502–23.

Madariaga, Salvador de. *On Hamlet.* 2d ed. London: Frank Cass, 1964.

Ornstein, Robert. *The Moral Vision of Jacobean Tragedy.* Madison: University of Wisconsin Press, 1960.

Partridge, Eric. *Shakespeare's Bawdy: A Literary and Psychological Essay and a Comprehensive Glossary.* London: Routledge and Kegan Paul, 1955.

Prosser, Eleanor. *Hamlet and Revenge.* Stanford: Stanford University Press, 1967.

Rabkin, Norman, ed. *Reinterpretations of Elizabethan Drama: Selected Papers from the English Institute.* New York: Columbia University Press, 1969.

Robertson, J. M. *"Hamlet" Once More.* London: Richard Cobden-Sanderson, 1923.

———. *The Problem of "Hamlet."* London: Allen and Unwin, 1919.

Rossi, Alfred. *Minneapolis Rehearsals: Tyrone Guthrie Directs 'Hamlet'.* Berkeley: University of California Press, 1970.

Rushton, William Lowes. *Shakespeare's Euphuism.* London: Longmans, Green, 1871.

Sacks, Claire, and Edgar Whan, eds. *Hamlet: Enter Critic.* New York: Appleton-Century-Crofts, 1960.

Santayana, George. *Interpretations of Poetry and Religion.* New York: Harper, 1957.

Schlegel, August Wilhelm von. *A Course of Lectures on Dramatic Art and Literature.* Translated by John Black, revised by A. J. W. Morrison. London: Henry G. Bohn, 1861.

Schucking, L. L. *Character Problems in Shakespeare's Plays.* 1922. New York: Peter Smith. 1948.

———. *The Meaning of Hamlet.* Translated by Graham Rawson. 1937. Reprint. New York: Barnes and Noble, 1966.

Shakespeare, William. *Hamlet.* Edited by Willard Farnham. The Pelican Shakespeare. Baltimore: Penguin Books, 1957.

———. *Hamlet.* Edited by Cyrus Hoy. New York: W. W. Norton, 1963.

———. *Hamlet.* Edited by Edward Hubler. The Signet Classic Shakespeare. New York: New American Library, 1963.

———. *Hamlet.* Edited by Harold Jenkins. The Arden Shakespeare. London: Methuen, 1982.

———. *Hamlet.* Edited by T. J. B. Spencer. The New Penguin Shakespeare. Harmondsworth: Penguin Books, 1980.

———. *Hamlet.* Edited by John Dover Wilson. The New Cambridge Shakespeare. Cambridge: Cambridge University Press, 1934.

Shattuck, Charles H. *The Hamlet of Edwin Booth.* Urbana: University of Illinois Press, 1969.

Shaw, George Bernard. *Shaw on Shakespeare: An Anthology of Bernard Shaw's Writings on the Plays and Production of Shakespeare.* Edited by Edwin Wilson. 1961. Reprint. Freeport, N.Y.: Books for Libraries Press, 1971.

Smith, Rebecca. "A Heart Cleft in Twain: The Dilemma of Shakespeare's Gertrude." In *The Woman's Part: Feminist Criticism of Shakespeare,* edited by Carolyn Ruth Swift Lenz, Gayle Greene, and Carol Thomas Neely, 194–210. Urbana: University of Illinois Press. 1980.

Spencer, Theodore. *Shakespeare and the Nature of Man.* New York: 1942.

Spevack, Marvin. *A Complete and Systematic Concordance to the Works of Shakespeare.* Vol. 3. Hildesheim: Georg Olms, 1968.

States, Bert O. "Horatio—Our Man in Elsinore: An Essay on Dramatic Logic." *South Atlantic Quarterly* 78(1979): 46–56.

Stoll, Elmer Edgar. *Art and Artifice in Shakespeare: A Study in Dramatic Contrast and Illusion.* Cambridge: Cambridge University Press, 1933.

———. *"Hamlet": An Historical and Comparative Study.* Minneapolis: University of Minnesota Press, 1919.

Stoppard, Tom. *Rosencrantz and Guildenstern Are Dead.* New York: Grove Press, 1967.

Taylor, Michael. "The Case of Rosencrantz and Guildenstern." *Dalhousie Review* 63(1983–84): 645–53.

Traversi, Derek. *An Approach to Shakespeare.* 3d ed. Vol. 2. New York: Anchor Books, 1969.

Waldock, A. J. A. *Hamlet: A Study in Critical Method.* 1931. Reprint. New York: AMS Press, 1973.

Walker, Roy. *The Time Is Out of Joint: A Study of Hamlet.* London: Andrew Dakers, 1948.

Werder, Karl. *The Heart of Hamlet's Mystery.* 1859–60. Translated by Elizabeth Wilder. New York: G. P. Putnam's Sons, 1907.

West, Robert Hunter. "King Hamlet's Ambiguous Ghost." *PMLA* (1955). Reprint in *Shakespeare and the Outer Mystery.* Lexington: University of Kentucky Press, 1968.

Willson, Robert F., Jr. *Shakespeare's Opening Scenes.* Salzburg Studies in English Literature 66. Salzburg: Institut für Englische Sprache und Literatur, Universität Salzburg, 1977.

Wilson, J. Dover. *What Happens in Hamlet.* Cambridge: Cambridge University Press, 1935.

Index